DURHAM MODERN LANGUAGE

GENERAL EDITOR

IAN MACPHERSON

SUBJECT EDITORS

GRAHAM E. RODMELL (FRENCH)

Prepositions in Modern Russian

Terence Wade

PRINTED FOR DURHAM MODERN LANGUAGES SERIES
BY
TITUS WILSON AND SON LTD.
28 HIGHGATE
KENDAL   CUMBRIA

CONTENTS

* This case is generally referred to in the text as the
  "locative".

PREFACE

The purpose of the monograph is to examine the meanings in contemporary Russian of 25 prepositions. The first fifteen of these are arranged in five sets of spatial 'opposites', the first in each set denoting, in its primary meaning, location at, the second motion towards and the third withdrawal from a particular place:

1. в	+ locative	в	+ accusative	из	+ genitive
2. на	+ locative	на	+ accusative	с	+ genitive
3. за	+ instrumental	за	+ accusative	из-за	+ genitive
4. под	+ instrumental	под	+ accusative	из-под	+ genitive
5. у	+ genitive	к	+ dative	от	+ genitive

The other 10 prepositions are arranged in alphabetical order:- для, до, над, о + accusative and prepositional, перед, по + accusative and dative, при, с + instrumental.

As far as possible the meanings of each preposition are dealt with in logical progression. The preposition's 'central' meaning is established and a maximum of other meanings derived from it. Thus:-

в городе	(in a place)
в автобусе	(in a vehicle)
в шляпе	(in clothing)
в панике	(in a state), etc.

Other meanings are grouped thematically. Thus, meanings of need:- недостаток в, необходимость в, нужда в, нуждаться в, etc., are grouped together, as are meanings of extent:- в крупном масштабе, в немалой мере, в такой степени, etc.

As many meanings as possible are enumerated for each preposition. A minimum of description is supplemented by a maximum of examples in the form of phrases, collocations and sentences, many abbreviated in the interests of economy, and all deriving from Soviet sources of the period since 1940.

Authors from whose work examples have been drawn include C. Aitmatov, V. Aksenov, S. Allilueva, N. Arzhak, B. Balter, N. Baranskaya, V. Bogomolov, V. Dorofeev, E. Dubrovin, V. Dudintsev, I. Ehrenburg, S. Gagarin, Yu. German, D. Granin, I. Grekova, V. Kaverin, E. Kazakevich, Yu. Kazakov, Yu. Khazanov, V. Kochetov, F. Koluntsev, A. Kuznetsov, L. Lench, L. Leonov, V. Lipatov, G. Markov, Yu. Nagibin, V. Nekrasov, V. Nikolaev, P. Nilin, V. Osipov, Yu. Otkupshchikov, V. Panova, B. Pasternak, K. Paustovsky, V. Rasputin, N. Reshetovskaya, V. Shukshin, A. Solzhenitsyn, V. Soloukhin, V. Tarsis, V. Tendryakov and A. Terts. Some of the examples are from Вокруг света, Известия, Литературная газета, Неделя and Огонек.

Secondary sources used include the Academy Grammar (2 volumes in 3 books, Moscow, 1960), the Academy Dictionary (17 volumes, Moscow, 1950-65), Словарь русского языка (4 volumes, Moscow, 1957-

61), S.I. Ozhegov, Словарь русского языка (10th edition, Moscow, 1973), V.V. Vinogradov, Русский язык. (Грамматическое учение о слове) (2nd edition, Moscow, 1972), M.V. Panov, editor, Морфология и синтаксис современного русского литературного языка (Moscow, 1968), I.M. Pul'kina, *Short Russian Reference Grammar* (Moscow, 1975), and specialist works on Russian prepositions by V. Bondarenko, D. Butorin, L. Vengerenko, E. Vladimirsky, L. Graudina, V. Itskovich and L. Katlinskaya, O. Ermakova, L. Zasorina, G. Zolotova, V. Matveeva, N. Leont'eva and S. Nikitina, I. Mal'tseva, U. Protopova, Ya. Roslovets, A. Spagis, A. Finkel' and E. Cherkasova, and also manuals by K. Gorbachevich, Изменение норм русского литературного языка (Leningrad, 1971), V. Itskovich, G.I. Mis'kevich and L. Skvortsov, editors, Грамматика и норма (Moscow, 1977), S. Pyatetskaya, Давайте познакомимся с русскими газетами (Moscow, 1974), D. Rozental', А как лучше сказать? (Moscow, 1979), L. Skvortsov, Правильно ли мы говорим по-русски? (Moscow, 1980), N. Shvedova, editor, Грамматика современного русского языка (Moscow, 1970), E. Yazovitsky, Говорите правильно (Moscow–Leningrad, 1964). M. Vsevolodova and Z. Parshukova's Способы выражения пространственных отношений (Moscow, 1968) was particularly helpful for the sections dealing with phrases in which either в or на may appear.

I am also grateful to those many native speakers of Russian who completed a questionnaire on this same point, and to M. Vyatyutnev and Dr. A. Shchukin, who arranged for colleagues in the Pushkin Institute, Moscow, to complete and return copies of the questionnaire, thus providing an invaluable insight into contemporary usage. I also wish to thank my editor, Professor W. Harrison, for many helpful suggestions, Mrs Ekaterina Young, for advising in the revision of my final draft and Miss Laura Pickard for her expert and careful typing in roman and Cyrillic.

Space unfortunately prevents the inclusion of a full bibliography. Those interested are referred to the bibliographies in the author's thesis, *Meanings of Extent and Purpose in Modern Russian Prepositions* (University of Strathclyde, 1977), volume 1, pp. 473-485, and *The Russian Preposition 'Do' and the Concept of Extent* (Birmingham, 1980), pp. 141-148. Some sources are referred to in the text of the monograph by the author's surname (Vsevolodova, Rozental', etc.) and page number.

***

NOTE that 'dependent item' denotes the noun governed by a preposition:-

в <u>городе</u>; под <u>арестом</u>; при <u>свете</u> ...

while 'dominant item' denotes the form which governs the prepositional phrase:-

<u>Плакать</u> с горя; <u>способен</u> к музыке; <u>ключ</u> от чемодана ...

University of Strathclyde   Terence Wade

I

В + LOCATIVE/PREPOSITIONAL CASE

(1) The preposition's central meaning is 'in', 'inside', 'at':-

В го́роде, в саду́   In the town, in the garden

Categories of dependent noun include:-

(a) the names of many buildings, structures, organisations (cf. на + locative 1(a), page 44):-

В аге́нтстве, акаде́мии,	In/at the agency, academy,
в апте́ке, ателье́ мод,	chemist's, fashion house,
в аэропорту́, бассе́йне,	airport, swimming pool,
библиоте́ке,	library,
в больни́це, буфе́те, ву́зе,	hospital, buffet, vuz*,
в галере́е, гастроно́ме,	gallery, grocer's,
гости́нице,	hotel,
во дворце́, в до́ме, институ́те,	palace, house, institute,
в кафе́, кио́ске, клу́бе,	cafe, kiosk, club,
в колхо́зе, ко́рпусе,	collective farm, block,
в консервато́рии, ла́гере,	(musical) conservatory, camp,
в магази́не, мастерско́й, метро́,	shop, workshop, underground,
в мили́ции, министе́рстве,	police station, ministry,
в музе́е, общежи́тии,	museum, hostel,
в парикма́херской,	hairdresser's,
в поликли́нике, порту́,	polyclinic, port,
рестора́не,	restaurant,
в санато́рии, совхо́зе,	sanatorium, state farm,
в спортза́ле, столо́вой, теа́тре,	gymnasium, canteen, theatre,
в те́хникуме,	technical college,
в типогра́фии, университе́те,	printing house, university,
в учи́лище,	college (trade, military, etc.),
в учрежде́нии, це́хе (цеху́),	institution, factory workshop,
в ци́рке, чита́льне, шко́ле	circus, reading room, school

(b) official organs and bodies:-

В комсомо́ле, па́ртии,	In the Komsomol, party,
в пионе́рской организа́ции,	Pioneer Organization,

*higher teaching establishment

в профсоюзе	trade union

(c) certain parts of buildings: (i) living accommodation (cf. на + locative 1(b) page 44):-

В ва́нной, вестибю́ле,	In the bathroom, vestibule,
в гости́ной, ко́мнате,	living-room, room,
коридо́ре,	corridor,
в но́мере, пере́дней, подва́ле,	hotel room, hall, basement,
в прихо́жей, спа́льне, туале́те	entrance, bedroom, toilet

(ii) academic accommodation (cf. на + locative 1(c), page 44-45):-

В аудито́рии, кла́ссе,	In the lecture room, class room,
в лаборато́рии	laboratory

(iii) administrative offices:-

В администра́ции, бухгалте́рии,	In administrative, accountancy,
в дире́кции	management offices

(iv) theatrical accommodation (cf. на + locative 1(d), page 45):-

В амфитеа́тре, аудито́рии,	In the back stalls, auditorium,
в бельэта́же, гардеро́бе, ло́же,	dress circle, cloakroom, box,
в парте́ре, фойе́	stalls, foyer

(d) geographical areas: (i) continents:-

В Австра́лии, А́зии, Аме́рике,	In Australia, Asia, America,
в А́фрике, Евро́пе	Africa, Europe

(ii) climatic zones and natural features:-

В Анта́рктике, А́рктике,	In the Antarctic, Arctic,
в гора́х, джу́нглях, лесу́,	mountains, jungle, forest,
в ми́ре, ни́зменности, океа́не,	world, lowlands, ocean,
в песка́х, пусты́не, снега́х,	sands, desert, snow(s),
в степи́, субтро́пиках,	steppe, sub-tropics,
в тайге́, тро́пиках, ту́ндре	taiga, tropics, tundra

(iii) countries, republics, regions:-

В СССР, А́нглии	In the USSR, England
В Донба́ссе, Крыму́, Сиби́ри,	In the Donbass, Crimea, Siberia,
Ла́твии	Latvia

(на Украи́не 'in the Ukraine', but в за́падной, Закарпа́тской Украи́не 'in the Western, Transcarpathian Ukraine')

(iv) islands with names ending in -ия:-

В Гренла́ндии, Исла́ндии,	In Greenland, Iceland,
в Но́вой Зела́ндии, Сици́лии	New Zealand, Sicily
В Сарди́нии расту́т оли́вковые	Olive trees grow in Sardinia
дере́вья	

(v) ranges of mountains with plural names:-

В А́льпах, А́ндах, Жигуля́х	In the Alps, Andes, Zhiguli
В Пирене́ях располо́жено	The state of Andorra is situated

государство Андо́рра   in the Pyrenees

Note: Тянь-Ша́нь (Tien Shan) appears with both в and на: в/на Тянь-Ша́не - other ranges with singular names combine with на unless qualified by an adjective (на Пами́ре, but в Восто́чном Пами́ре). However, Кавка́з (Caucasus) appears only with на: на Кавка́зе, на Восто́чном Кавка́зе.

(vi) administrative areas:-

В кра́е, о́бласти, о́круге   In a krai, oblast, okrug

(vii) towns:-

В Москве́, Ки́еве, Ло́ндоне   In Moscow, Kiev, London

(viii) certain city regions (cf. на + locative 1(e) viii page 46):-

В Замоскворе́чье, Заря́дье,   In Zamoskvorech'e, Zaryad'e,
в Изма́йлово, Лефо́ртове,   Izmailovo, Lefortovo,
в Оста́нкино, Подмоско́вье,   Ostankino, Podmoskov'e,
Черёмушках   Cheremushki

(ix) certain parts of a town (cf. на + locative 1(e) ix page 46):-

В переу́лке, предме́стье,   In a side-street, suburb,
в при́городе, прое́зде, тупике́,   suburb, passage, cul-de-sac,
в це́нтре, у́личке (usually in   centre, small street
combination with у́зкая
'narrow')

(2) The dependent noun denotes a mode of transport (cf. на + locative 2, page 48). The dominant form denotes travelling:-

Я е́хал в авто́бусе, в ли́фте   I was travelling in a bus,
      going in a lift
Лете́ть в самолёте   To fly in an aircraft

or other actions and states:-

Все сиде́ли в маши́нах   Everyone was sitting in the cars
Уро́ки я вы́учила в тролле́йбусе   I did my homework in the trolley-
      bus

(3) The dependent noun may denote a spatial point:-

Она́ вста́ла во главе́ стола́ (cf.   She stood up at the head of the
во главе́ предприя́тия 'at the   table
head of an enterprise')
Ко́йка со спаса́тельным кру́гом в   A bunk with a life-belt at its
голова́х   head
В изно́жье его́ крова́ти виси́т   A card hangs at the foot of his
ка́рточка   bed
Кио́ск стоя́л в нача́ле   The kiosk stood at the beginning
пусты́нной у́лицы   of a deserted street

В хвосте́ о́череди	At the tail-end of the queue

The spatial point may be a part of the body:-

Но́ги сгиба́лись в коле́нях	His legs bent at the knees
Со́гнутые в локтя́х ру́ки	Arms bent at the elbows
Хала́т стя́нут в та́лии пояско́м от плаща́	The gown is drawn together at the waist with a coat-belt
Ру́ки и но́ги бы́ли схва́чены в лоды́жках и запя́стьях	His arms and legs were pinioned at the ankles and wrists

(4) The dependent noun denotes an article of clothing, footwear, etc.:-

Он в боти́нках, джи́нсах, носка́х, в очка́х, сви́тере, ша́почке	He is wearing shoes, jeans, socks, glasses, a sweater, a cap

(5) A number of nouns combine with в and/or на, depending on context:-

Во́здух: в is preferred in the meanings 'up in the air', 'pervading the air':-

Стреми́тельный разбе́г — и самолёт в во́здухе	A swift take-off run and the plane is in the air
В во́здухе пови́с за́пах табака́	A smell of tobacco hung in the air

На is preferred in the meaning 'out in the open air':-

Весь день прово́дят на во́здухе	They spend all day in the open air

Высота́: в is preferred when quantification is not implied:-

В прозра́чной высоте́	In the translucent heights

На is preferred when quantification is expressed or implied:-

На высоте́ четырёх киломе́тров, на э́той высоте́	At a height of 4 kilometres, at this height

Глаз: Either preposition is possible in the context of tears:-

В/на глаза́х показа́лись слёзы	Tears appeared in her eyes

В is preferred when the dominant form denotes emotion:-

Выраже́ние страда́ния в её глаза́х	An expression of suffering in her eyes

when the dependent noun denotes 'opinion':-

Каки́м болва́ном я вы́глядел в её глаза́х	What a blockhead I must have appeared in her eyes

На is preferred in the meaning 'on the surface of the eye':-

Конта́ктные ли́нзы, кото́рые остаю́тся на глазу́ ме́сяцами	Contact lenses, which stay in the eyes for months on end

and in the meanings 'in the presence of', 'swiftly':-

Города́ рожда́ются уже́ на на́ших глаза́х	Towns spring up before our very eyes

Глубина́: в is preferred when quantification is not implied:-

В морско́й глубине́, в океа́нских глуби́нах	In the depths of the sea, in the ocean depths

and to denote 'at the back, bottom', etc.:-

В глубине́ за́ла, в глубине́ ле́са, в глубине́ са́да	At the back of the hall, in the depths of the forest, at the bottom of the garden

На is preferred when quantification is expressed or implied:-

На глубине́ трёх сантиме́тров	At a depth of three centimetres

Двор: в is preferred when reference is to an area surrounded by houses or a fence, while на implies 'outside'. The meanings may overlap. Vsevolodova: 66 describes the prepositions as synonyms in:-

Де́ти игра́ют во/на дворе́	The children are playing in the yard outside

В is used to refer to a particular yard:-

Во дворе́ до́ма но́мер 50	In the yard of house no. 50
Во дворе́ бы́ло две и́ли три покры́шки	There were two or three outer covers in the yard

На is used in reference to climatic conditions:-

На дворе́ зима́	It is winter outside

when the type of area is specified by an adjective which implies spaciousness, either directly:-

На широ́ком дворе́	In a broad yard
cf. В кро́хотном дво́рике	In a tiny yard

or indirectly:-

На колхо́зном дворе́, ко́нном дворе́, на ско́тном дворе́, шко́льном дворе́	In the farm yard, stable yard, cattle yard, school yard
На за́днем дворе́ был като́к	There was a rink in the back yard

Кварти́ра: Either preposition is possible when residence is indicated:-

Жить в/на но́вой кварти́ре	To live in a new apartment

Either is also possible in contexts of visiting:-

Ты не́ был у него́ в/на кварти́ре? Haven't you been at his flat?

and when the dominant word denotes activity:-

Исто́рия с Ню́рой произошла́ в/на но́вой кварти́ре	The incident involving Nyura occurred at the new flat

В is preferred when atmosphere, conditions, etc., are indicated:-

В кварти́ре цари́ла тишь	Quiet reigned in the apartment

and when components are indicated:-

В э́той кварти́ре три ко́мнаты	There are three rooms in this flat

На is preferred in the meaning 'temporarily', 'at someone else's place':-

Мой друг пока́ на ча́стной кварти́ре	My friend is staying in a private flat for the time being

According to Vsevolodova: 70, на кварти́ре can be synonymous with до́ма. Here is an example from a technical reader:-

Но́вый аппара́т мо́жно бу́дет испо́льзовать не то́лько в кли́нике, но и на кварти́ре	It will be possible to use the new apparatus not only in the clinic, but also at home

Коне́ц: Either preposition may be used to denote the end(s) of an object:-

Я по́мню ма́му в/на конце́ перро́на в её чёрных ту́флях	I remember mother standing at the end of the platform in her black shoes

and when the dependent noun combines with тот and certain other qualifiers:-

В/на да́льнем конце́ по́ля, противополо́жном конце́ стола́, том конце́ ко́мнаты	At the far end of the field, the opposite end of the table, the other end of the room
Мы сиде́ли в/на ра́зных конца́х стола́	We sat at opposite ends of the table

В is preferred in contexts involving the end of a space:-

В конце́ у́лицы, коридо́ра	At the end of a street, corridor

Коню́шня: The prepositions are synonymous (Vsevolodova: 67) in:-

Ло́шади стоя́т в/на коню́шне	The horses are standing in the stable

Крова́ть: Both prepositions are found in contexts of sleeping, lying in bed:-

Все давно́ вста́ли, а ты ещё в крова́ти!	Everyone got up long ago, and you are still in bed!
Я сказа́л, чтобы он спал на мое́й крова́ти	I said he should sleep in my bed

B is used in other contexts denoting 'under the bedclothes':-

Лежа́ть. в крова́ти   To be laid up, confined to bed

Я с де́тства чита́л в крова́ти   Since childhood I had been in the habit of reading in bed

Ha may indicate location on top of the bedclothes:-

Врач сиде́л на крова́ти   The doctor was sitting on the bed

and is preferred when emphasis is laid on juxtaposition or contrast:-

Размести́лись в одно́й из ко́мнат
 - Са́ша на крова́ти, Ва́ня на
дива́не

They settled down in one of the rooms - Sasha on the bed, Vanya on the sofa

Ку́хня: Either preposition is used to denote whereabouts, activity, atmosphere, etc.:-

Холоди́льник стои́т в/на ку́хне   The refrigerator stands in the kitchen

В/на ку́хне станови́лось жа́рко   It was getting hot in the kitchen

Она́ что́-то в/на ку́хне дова́ри-
вала

She was finishing off cooking something in the kitchen

Rozenthal': 105 quotes a snatch of dialogue:- -Эти разгово́ры вы слы́шали в ку́хне? -Да, на ку́хне. Ha is commoner in colloquial usage.

Ме́сто: Both prepositions are possible in non-spatial contexts:-

Так в/на са́мом интере́сном
 ме́сте оборва́лся разгово́р

And so the conversation broke off at the most interesting place

though в seems commoner in the plural:-

В ну́жных места́х де́лал па́узы   He paused at the relevant points

Either preposition is possible in combination with certain adjectives:-

В/на но́вом ме́сте, обы́чном
ме́сте, опа́сном, тру́дном
ме́сте

At a new place, in the usual place, in a dangerous, difficult spot

and in the following (Vsevolodova: 78):-

Он постоя́л в/на одно́м ме́сте,
пото́м в/на друго́м

He stood for a while at one place, then at another

B is preferred when the dependent item denotes part(s) of a whole:-

Кни́га по́рвана в одно́м ме́сте   The book is torn in one place

when the dependent noun denotes a three-dimensional area:-

Фотобума́гу я держу́ в тёмном   I keep the photographic paper in месте   a dark place

when the meaning of the prepositional phrase is 'together':-

Все вещи нужно собрать в одном месте	Everything must be collected in one spot

when the dependent item denotes 'area(s), locality(ies)':-

Лагерь разбили в чудесном месте	They pitched camp in a marvellous spot

when the meaning is 'the same':-

Я встречал его всегда в одном месте	I always met him at the same place

when the noun combines with certain adjectives (Vsevolodova: 77) :-

В глубоком, другом месте, в общественном месте, узком месте	At a deep place, elsewhere, in a public place, a narrow place
В разных местах выпадает свой снег	Different snow falls in different places

На is preferred to indicate 'in the proper place':-

Все мои вещи лежат на месте	All my things are in their proper place

in the meaning 'without moving from the spot':-

Стоять на месте, решить на месте	To stand still, decide on the spot

when the dependent noun is qualified by a possessive:-

Я сижу на твоём месте	I am sitting in your place

when the context denotes activity:-

Поймать на месте преступления	To catch red-handed

when the context denotes former whereabouts:-

Деньги лежат на прежнем месте	The money is lying where it was

or replacement:-

На месте пустырей выросли жилые кварталы	Where there was waste ground blocks of flats have sprung up

when the dependent noun denotes a flat area:-

На ровном месте высился камень	A rock towered up on a level stretch of ground

when the dependent noun is qualified by an ordinal numeral:-

Среди причин, на втором месте назывались жилищные условия	Among causes mentioned, housing conditions were in second place

when the context denotes preferred conduct:-

На вашем месте я уехал бы	If I were you I would leave

when the noun combines with certain adjectives:-

На рабочем месте, мелком месте	At one's work place, at a shallow place

when the noun denotes 'provinces':-

Первый тур проводится на местах	The first round is held in the provinces

Море: Both prepositions are used in the context of natural phenomena:-

Ураган в/на Жёлтом море	A hurricane in the Yellow Sea

В is used in reference to fauna, flora and other submarine items:-

Эти рыбы водятся в Чёрном море	These fish are found in the Black Sea

when the prepositional phrase implies a sea voyage:-

Корабль уже давно в море	The ship has been under way for some time

and in certain set phrases:-

Далеко в море, в открытом море	Far out to sea, in the open sea

На is preferred where the sea appears as a place of work:-

На реке тяжелее, чем на море	It is harder working on a river than at sea

when reference is to events on the surface of the sea:-

Приключения на суше и на море	Adventures on land and sea

В may be used to indicate the whereabouts of an island, etc.:-

Остров Сафарьева затерялся в Охотском море	Safar'ev Island is a mere dot in the Sea of Okhotsk

Небо: Either preposition is possible in the context of natural phenomena:-

Огромное солнце в/на чистом небе	An enormous sun in the clear sky

В is preferred when reference is to birds, aircraft, sounds, etc.:-

Варя увидела в небе 2 вертолёта	Varya saw 2 helicopters in the sky
В небе послышался рокот	A low rumble was heard in the sky

Огород: Both prepositions are used to denote growth, activity, etc.:-

Кири́лл был в/на огоро́де	Kirill was in the market garden
Мы поло́ли в/на огоро́де	We were weeding in the market garden

Окно́: в is preferred when the context denotes 'framed, visible':-

В окне́ показа́лась его́ голова́	His head appeared in the window

На is preferred when the dependent noun means 'window sill':-

На окне́ стоя́ли цветы́	There were flowers on the sill

and in the context of draperies:-

На о́кнах розове́ли занаве́ски	There were pink curtains at the windows

Отделе́ние: в is preferred for non-academic contexts:-

В почто́вом отделе́нии, в отделе́нии мили́ции	In the postal department, at the police station

На is preferred for academic contexts:-

Он у́чится на славя́нском отделе́нии	He studies at the Slavonic Department

По́ле: в is preferred where по́ле is distinguished from other topographical features (forest, marsh, etc.) or is contrasted with the village and work in the fields is implied:-

Я ви́дел его́ далеко́ в по́ле	I saw him far off in the fields
В дере́вне пу́сто, все в по́ле	The village is deserted, everyone is in the fields

Both prepositions are possible in referring to water, floods etc.:-

В/на поля́х лежа́ла вода́	Water lay on the fields

На по́ле denotes a particular plot:-

На по́ле стоя́л тра́ктор	In the field stood a tractor
На поля́х рабо́тали лю́ди	People were working in the fields

На is also used when an adjective specifies a crop:-

На овся́ном, карто́фельном по́ле	In a field of oats, potatoes

and in military and sporting contexts:-

Он поги́б на по́ле бо́я	He died on the battlefield
На ле́тном, футбо́льном по́ле	On the flying field, the football field

Note also:-

На поля́х	In the margin

Постель: в is preferred in the meanings 'under the bedclothes', 'confined to bed', etc.:-

Она́ уже́ тре́тий день лежи́т в посте́ли	This is the third day she has been laid up

while на often implies 'on top of the bedclothes':-

На посте́ли, укры́тый шине́лью, лежа́л пожило́й челове́к	On the bed, covered by a great-coat, lay a middle-aged man

Разве́дка: в appears in the context of military operations and intelligence:-

Зо́рге рабо́тал в разве́дке	Sorge worked in intelligence
В боево́й разве́дке, в контрразве́дке	On combat reconnaissance, on counter intelligence

На appears in the context of prospecting:-

Он рабо́тает на разве́дке не́фти	He works in oil prospecting

Рука́: в is used when the dependent noun means 'hand':-

У Арсе́ния в рука́х была́ аво́ська с тремя́ буты́лками	Arsenii was holding a string bag containing 3 bottles

На is used when the dependent noun means 'arm':-

На одно́й руке́ у неё ребёнок	She is holding a child in one arm
Она́ подошла́ с Ви́тькой на рука́х	She came up with Vit'ka in her arms

Свет: в is used when the noun means 'light':-

В жёлтом све́те фонаре́й ещё толпи́лись па́рни и де́вушки	The young fellows and girls still crowded in the yellow light of the lamps

Note the figurative: в све́те но́вых откры́тий 'in the light of recent discoveries'. На is used in the meaning 'world':-

Чуде́с на све́те не быва́ет	Miracles do not happen in this world

and in contexts where light is used for the purposes of examination:-

Осма́тривала оде́жду на свету́, перед окно́м	She was examining the clothes in the light, in front of the window

Середи́на: Either preposition is used for the centre of an area:-

Тра́ктор стоя́л в/на середи́не по́ля	The tractor stood in the middle of the field

В середи́не denotes enclosure, encirclement, 'in between':-

В середи́не толпы́	In the middle of a crowd
Рома́н в середи́не, де́вушки	Roman in the middle, the girls at

по края́м   the sides

Сквер: Both prepositions are used, though Vsevolodova: 39 regards на as more normal:-

Пото́м мы сиде́ли в скве́ре	Then we sat in the public garden
Просиде́л я на скве́ре всё остально́е вре́мя	All the rest of the time I sat in the public garden

Село́: В is used when the noun means 'village':-

В на́шем селе́ постро́или но́вую шко́лу	A new school has been built in our village

На is used when the noun denotes 'country area(s)':-

Роль интеллиге́нции на селе́ о́чень велика́	The intelligentsia's role in country areas is very great

Сту́дия: в is preferred in the following combinations:-

В о́перной, театра́льной сту́дии, в сту́дии худо́жника	In the operatic, theatrical studio, an artist's studio

На is now used in the standard language in the following combinations, originally restricted to the speech of professionals in these fields:-

На радиосту́дии, телесту́дии	At the radio, TV studio
Фильм дубли́рован на киносту́дии	The film has been dubbed at the film studio

Суд: в is used when the noun denotes 'court room':-

В суде́ сего́дня многолю́дно	The court is crowded today

Either preposition can be used when the noun denotes 'court session':-

Этот адвока́т произнёс в/на суде́ блестя́щую речь	This barrister made a brilliant speech at the trial

Таре́лка: в is used to indicate a deep plate, на to indicate a flat plate:-

В таре́лке суп	There is soup in the plate
Хлеб на таре́лке	The bread is on the plate

У́лица: на у́лице is the norm. The phrase now also rivals на дворе́ in the meaning 'outside':- на у́лице моро́з 'it is frosty outside'. В may be found when the noun is qualified by у́зкая:-

Мы остана́вливались в у́зких у́лицах	We would stop in the narrow streets

Флот: Either preposition is possible, though на still tends to be termed professional usage (see, for example, Ozhegov and the Academy Dictionary):-

Мой брат слу́жит в/на фло́те	My brother is in the navy

Шáхта: в implies 'down the mine', на 'at the mine':-

Он рабóтает в шáхте	He works at the coal face
Он рабóтает на шáхте	He works at the colliery

(6) Some verbs combine with в + locative or accusative, sometimes with no apparent change in meaning:-

Он усéлся в крéсле, в крéсло	He settled in an armchair.

Elsewhere the locative may denote an area of comparatively larger size:-

Заставлял себя запирáть в кабинéте (cf. зáпер бумáги в ящик 'locked the papers in a drawer')	He would have himself locked in his study
Меня помести́ли в одинóчной кáмере (cf. помести́ть в контéйнер 'to place in a container')	I was placed in a solitary cell
Хотéла сесть в послéднем ряду́ (cf. сади́лся в крéсло 'he would sit in an armchair')	She wanted to sit in the back row
Дёма спря́тал в тýмбочке рецéпт (cf. спря́тал стилó во внýтренний кармáшек 'hid the stylo in his inside pocket')	Dema hid the prescription in his bed-side table

Cf. also появля́ться 'to appear' and the more official явля́ться:-

Появи́лась в квартúре с чемодáном	She appeared in the flat with her suitcase
Яви́лась в суд	She appeared before the court

Other verbs also combine with the locative despite apparently directional meanings:-

Перебирáлся на лóдке на другóй бéрег и исчезáл в лесý	He would cross to the opposite bank and disappear in the forest
Распахнýла дверь в кóмнату и скры́лась в ней	She flung open the door to the room and disappeared into it
В аэропортý гóрода Ми́нска приземли́лся самолёт из Москвы́	An aircraft from Moscow landed at Minsk airport

Cf. also:-

Они́ шли все в однóм направлéнии	They were all going in the same direction

(7) The dependent noun denotes a physical state or condition:-

В бе́дности, в (бес)поря́дке,	In poverty, in (dis)order,
в испра́вности, в перепи́ске,	in good repair, in correspondence,
в пути́ (cf. на обра́тном пути́ 'on the way back'),	en route,
в распоряже́нии, в состоя́нии,	at the disposal of, in a state,
в сохра́нности,	in a good state of preservation,
в ссы́лке, в це́лости	in exile, intact
В нево́ле ожесточа́ются их сердца́	Their hearts become savage in captivity
Она́ сама́ ви́дела, что колхо́з в тру́дном положе́нии	She could see for herself that the farm was in a bad way

or a mental state or condition:-

В восто́рге, в волне́нии,	In delight, in excitement,
в гне́ве, в го́ре,	in anger, in sorrow,
в заду́мчивости, в му́ке,	deep in thought, in torment,
в настрое́нии, в ожида́нии,	in a mood, in expectation,
в отча́янии, в поры́ве ...,	in despair, in a fit of ...,
в расте́рянности, в сомне́нии	in confusion, in doubt
В каки́х вы с ним отноше́ниях?	How do you get on with him?
Я не оста́влю его́ в поко́е	I shall not leave him alone

There may be a nuance of cause:-

В па́нике убежа́л из ко́мнаты	He ran out of the room in a panic
В у́жасе она́ зажа́ла у́ши	She pressed her hands over her ears in horror

(8) The dependent noun may denote the form of presentation:-

Са́хар в куска́х	Lump sugar

There are abstract equivalents:-

Выполне́ние норм в проце́нтах	Fulfilment of norms in percentages
Нра́вится ему́ те́хника - не в тео́рии, а на пра́ктике	He likes technology, not in theory, but in practice

Note also в оригина́ле (в по́длиннике) 'in the original', в перево́де 'in translation'

(9) The prepositional phrase means 'covered in', 'abounding in', etc:-

Па́льцы у меня́ в цара́пинах	My fingers are covered in scratches
Всё по́ле в цвета́х	The whole field is a mass of flowers

Околыш был весь в извести	His cap-band was covered in lime
Здание всё в лесах	The building is in scaffolding
Небо в тучах	The sky is dark with storm clouds

Other phrases include:-

В веснушках, заплатах, в инее, краске, крови, кляксах, в мусоре, порезах, поту, прыщах, в пуху, пятнах, синяках, снегу, в ссадинах, трещинах	Covered in freckles, patches, hoar-frost, paint, blood, blots, garbage, cuts, sweat, pimples, fluff, stains, bruises, snow, abrasions, cracks

(10) The phrase denotes a professional, social or other group:-

Я был в гостях у одного художника (cf. матч в гостях 'away match')	I was visiting a certain artist
В девках останешься	You will be left on the shelf
В живых оставался капитан судна	The captain of the ship survived
Никогда в домработницах не служила	She had never worked as a servant

(11) The phrase denotes distance (cf. за + accusative case 2, pages 77-78):-

В пяти километрах от ГЭС лежало большое озеро	A large lake was situated five kilometres from the power station

especially where specific orientation is indicated elsewhere in the sentence:-

Мы выгрузились в лесу, в 120 километрах западнее Москвы	We debussed in a forest, 120 kilometres to the west of Moscow

and when distance is expressed in temporal terms:-

Школа минутах в десяти от нашего дома	The school is about ten minutes from our house

or by the noun отдаление:-

Он садился в отдалении, в некотором отдалении, в почтительном отдалении	He would sit down some distance away, at a certain distance, a respectful distance

(12) Temporal expressions:-

  (a) the preposition combines with век 'century', год 'year',

месяц 'month', тысячелетие 'millennium' (cf. also в + accusative
14(c) and (d) pages 34-35, and на + accusative 25(a) page 61):-

В этом, прошлом, будущем месяце, году, веке	This, last, next month, year, century
В сентябре прошлого года она дважды преодолела Ла-Манш	Last September she crossed the Channel twice
Овладение в следующем году частью Финляндии	The capture of part of Finland in the following year
В 1920-1921 годах в России не было написано ни одного романа	Not one novel was written in Russia in 1920-21
В 1960-х годах (also: в 1960-е годы cf. в + accusative 14(c) page 34)	In the sixties
В 21 веке, в первом тысячелетии	In the 21st century, in the first millennium

Note also the following temporal usage:-

В половине второго разгримировался	He took his grease-paint off at 1.30
Явилась в восьмом часу утра	She appeared between 7 and 8 a.m.
В первых числах июля	In the first days of July
В сумерках я возвращался к себе	I would return home at dusk
В нынешней пятилетке на эти нужды расходуется 100 миллиардов рублей	During the present five-year-plan 100,000,000,000 roubles are being expended on these requirements

(b) the preposition combines with прошлое, настоящее, будущее
'past', 'present', 'future':-

В далёком прошлом этот холм представлял собой курган	In the distant past this hill was a burial mound

(c) it combines with начало, середина, конец 'beginning', 'middle', 'end':-

Не в самом начале, не в самом конце, а где-то в середине произнёс короткую речь	He delivered a short speech not at the very beginning, not at the very end, but somewhere in the middle

Note also:- в конце концов 'finally', 'eventually'.

(d) it combines with the names of intervals, parts of processes,
and other indeterminate time segments:-

В антракте мы ели мороженое	In the interval we ate ice-cream

Находи́ться в о́тпуске	To be on holiday
В переры́ве я не обе́даю (also в переры́в)	I do not have lunch at break-time
В тре́тьем пери́оде сове́тские хоккеи́сты забили три го́ла	In the third period the Soviet ice-hockey team scored 3 goals
Во второ́й полови́не, в после́дней че́тверти 19-го ве́ка	In the second half, final quarter of the 19th century
В преддве́рии собы́тий	On the threshold of events
В ны́нешнем сезо́не мужски́е га́лстуки ста́нут не́сколько у́же	In the present season men's ties will become somewhat narrower
Во второ́м та́йме сове́тские спортсме́ны одержа́ли втору́ю побе́ду	In the second half the Soviet team won their second victory
В после́днем ту́ре на́ши шахмати́стки раздели́ли пе́рвенство	In the final round our women chess players shared the championship

(e) the dependent noun denotes stages in a life:-

Приуча́ться к ко́фе в её во́зрасте нежела́тельно	It is undesirable to get used to drinking coffee at her age
Сни́тся ли мне э́то всё опя́ть, как в де́тстве?	Am I dreaming it all over again, as in my childhood?
В мо́лодости, ста́рости, младе́нчестве	In youth, old age, babyhood

(f) the dependent noun denotes 'event', 'occasion':-

Флаг поднима́ют в осо́бых слу́чаях	The flag is hoisted on special occasions

(13) The dependent noun or pronoun defines the context of dominant forms such as вина́ 'guilt', зада́ча 'task', ра́зница 'difference':-

Беда́ в том, что она́ меня́ сли́шком лю́бит	The trouble is that she loves me too much
Нет, де́ло не в во́зрасте!	No, age is not the point!
В чём причи́на популя́рности дельтапланери́зма?	What is the reason for the popularity of hang-gliding?
Вопро́с в том, соотве́тствуют ли фа́кты действи́тельности	The question is whether the facts correspond to reality
Секре́т и́менно в э́том: поме́ньше смотре́ть на теневы́е сто́роны	The secret is this: to look less on the black side

The verbs заключа́ться, состоя́ть may be 'understood' in such constructions, cf.:-

Поня́тие ве́чности всегда́ заключа́лось для меня́ в друго́м	For me the concept of eternity always consisted in something different

(14) The dependent noun denotes the object of:-

  (a) 'guilt', 'suspicion', etc.:-

Аресто́ван по подозре́нию в кра́же	Arrested on suspicion of theft
Всех шестеры́х обвиня́ла во взры́ве комендату́ры	She accused all six of blowing up the commandant's office
Я бы никогда́ в э́том не призна́лся	I would never have confessed to that

Other items include:-

Вини́ть в, вино́вный/винова́тый в, обвине́ние в, подозрева́ть в, провиня́ться в, призна́ние в, раска́иваться в, упрека́ть в	To blame for, guilty of, an accusation of, to suspect of, to be guilty of, a confession of, to repent of, to reproach with

  (b) 'confidence', 'conviction', 'verification', 'doubt':-

Врачи́ усомни́лись в диа́гнозе	The doctors cast doubt on the diagnosis
Зри́тели могли́ удостове́риться в пустоте́ сундука́	The audience could testify to the emptiness of the trunk
Кля́тва в дру́жбе	A vow of friendship
Он уве́рен в себе́	He is sure of himself

Other items include:-

Кля́сться в (ве́рности), разочаро́вываться в, разуверя́ться в, распи́сываться в, сомнева́ться в, сомне́ние в, убежда́ть(ся) в, убежде́ние в, уверя́ть в, уаре́ние в	To swear (loyalty), to be disappointed in, to lose faith in, to sign for, to doubt, doubt in, to convince (oneself) of, conviction of, to assure of, assurance of

  (c) 'need':-

В нас нужда́лась па́ртия и госуда́рство	Party and state needed us

Other items include:-

Недоста́ток в,	Lack of,

необходи́мость в, нужда́ в, потре́бность в	necessity for, need for, requirement for

The verb отка́зывать can also be related to this category:-

Ты что, отказа́л ей в по́мощи?	You mean you denied aid to her?

(d) comprehension:-

Он ничего́ не понима́ет в жи́вописи	He understands nothing about painting
Отдава́ть себе́ отчёт в опа́сности	To realise the danger
Како́й ура́лец не зна́ет толк в ка́мне?	What inhabitant of the Urals does not know about stones?
В таки́х дела́х Инка разбира́лась	Inka knew about affairs of this kind

(e) 'involvement', 'participation':-

Выступа́ть в о́пере	To appear in an opera
В опера́ции уча́ствуют о́коло 200 челове́к	About 200 people are taking part in the operation
Тро́е подсуди́мых получи́ли по 5 лет за соуча́стие в уби́йстве	The three accused got five years each for complicity in the murder

(15) The dependent noun denotes 'measure', 'extent':-

Таки́е вопро́сы должны́ реша́ться в госуда́рственном масшта́бе	Such questions should be tackled on a national scale
В кру́пном масшта́бе, ма́ссовом масшта́бе	On a large, mass scale
В доста́точной ме́ре, ма́лой ме́ре, в како́й-то ме́ре, по́лной ме́ре, в ре́дкой мере, ра́вной ме́ре	In sufficient measure, small measure, some measure, full measure, unusual measure, equal measure
Приро́да изу́чена в тако́й сте́пени, что неожи́данности вряд ли возмо́жны	Nature has been studied to such a degree that surprises are hardly possible

Cf. до + genitive case (12). В is preferred in combination with сте́пень in the lower ranges of extent:-

В сла́бой, ма́лой сте́пени	To a reduced, small extent

and in the comparative range:-

В бо́льшей (вы́сшей) сте́пени, в ме́ньшей сте́пени, в ра́зной, одина́ковой сте́пени	To a greater extent, a lesser extent, varying, identical degrees

Тра́вкин ни в мале́йшей сте́пени не дога́дывался о её и́стинных чу́вствах

Travkin did not divine her true feelings in the slightest

(16) The confirmatory phrase в са́мом де́ле:-

Иску́сство должно́ нести́ в себе́ (и в са́мом де́ле несёт) черты́ национа́льной принадле́жности

Art should bear within itself (and in fact does bear) features of national identity

(17) The phrase в прису́тствии:-

В её прису́тствии мо́жно бы́ло молча́ть

One could be silent in her prescence

II

B + ACCUSATIVE CASE

(1) The dominant form implies motion to or into a place or area. See в + locative (1) for the types of place involved:-

Еду в аэропо́рт	I am driving to the airport
Она́ уе́хала в колхо́з	She has left for the farm
Она́ пришла́ в мили́цию	She arrived at the police station
Он откры́л дверь в спа́льню	He opened the door to the bedroom
Ко́стя по́дал в институ́т	Kostya applied for the institute

Note also: я позвони́л ему́ в Ки́ев 'I rang him in Kiev'

(2) The dependent noun denotes a vehicle or other mode of transport (cf. в + locative 2, page 11 and на + accusative 2, page 55) :-

Сади́ться в авто́бус, ло́дку, маши́ну, в по́езд, самолёт, са́ни, трамва́й	To get into a bus, a boat, a car, a train, a plane, a sledge, a tram
Она́ се́ла в такси́	She got into a taxi

(3) The dominant form denotes 'dressing', 'dressed' (cf. в + locative 4, page 12):-

Он оде́т в чёрное	He is dressed in black
Он переоде́лся в гражда́нский костю́м	He changed into civilian clothes

(4) Some nouns combine with either в or на + accusative case, sometimes with a difference in meaning, compare:-

Самолёты в во́здух не подня́ть	It is impossible to get the aircraft into the air

and:-

Выходи́ть на во́здух	To go out into the open air,
Сесть на коня́ и е́хать в по́ле	To mount a horse and ride into the fields

and:-

Он е́здит на по́ле бо́я	He rides to the field of battle,
Лечь в посте́ль и усну́ть	To get into bed and go to sleep

and:-

Он сел на посте́ль	He sat down on the bed,
Брать в ру́ки	To take in one's hands

and:-

Она́ подхвати́ла ма́льчика на́ руки	She gathered the boy up in her arms,
Всё вре́мя перехо́дят из те́ни в свет	They keep moving from the shadow into the light

and:-

Появи́ться на свет	To come into the world

The above examples are representative only. For a detailed categorisation of phrases and contexts, see в + locative (5).

(5) Note also:-

Входи́ть в дом	To go into the house

but:-

Брать рабо́ту на́ дом	To take work home,
Идти́ в го́ру	To go uphill

but:-

Забра́ться на́ гору	To climb a hill
Шепну́ть на́ ухо (в is less usual: шепну́ть пря́мо в у́хо 'to whisper directly into someone's ear')	To whisper in someone's ear

(6) See в + locative (6) for a section on dominant forms which combine with в + locative and в + accusative, page 21.

(7) The dependent noun denotes a state (cf. в + locative 7, p22):-

Приходи́ть в бе́шенство, в восто́рг, в негодова́ние, приходи́ть в отча́яние, приходи́ть в созна́ние,	To become enraged, delighted, indignant, to despair, to come round,

приходи́ть в у́жас	to be horrified

Приводи́ть в бе́шенство,	To madden,
в восто́рг,	delight,
приводи́ть в исполне́ние,	to put into effect,
приводи́ть в ... настрое́ние,	to put in a ... mood,
приводи́ть в отча́яние,	to drive to despair,
приводи́ть в поря́док,	to put in order,
приводи́ть в смуще́ние,	to embarrass,
приводи́ть в соотве́тствие с,	to bring into accord with,
приводи́ть в у́жас, в я́рость	to horrify, enrage

Впада́ть в уны́ние,	To become depressed,
впада́ть в сомне́ние,	to be assailed by doubts,
впада́ть в па́нику	to panic

Погружа́ться в разду́мье	To be plunged in reverie

Вступа́ть в брак, вступа́ть в разгово́р	To marry, to enter into conversation

Э́тот ход привёл их в замеша́тельство	This move confounded them

Ты его́ в курс де́ла не вводи́л	You did not put him in the picture

Иногда́ я впада́л в отча́яние	Sometimes I would despair

Фа́кты ста́вят в тупи́к экспе́ртов	The facts nonplus the experts

Ма́льчика привели́ в созна́ние	They brought the boy round

(8) The dependent noun denotes the result of conversion, disintegration:-

Превраща́ть в разва́лины	To reduce to ruins

Разрыва́ть в клочки́	To tear to shreds

Разбива́ть в ще́пки (в пух и прах)	To smash to smithereens

or an arrangement resulting from an action or movement:-

Сжима́ть па́льцы в кула́к	To clench one's fist

Скла́дывать в ку́чу	To pile in a heap

Уса́живаться в круг, располага́ться в ряд	To sit in a circle, arrange oneselves in a row

Мота́ть шерсть в клубки́	To wind wool into balls

(9) The dependent noun denotes 'disposal', 'utilisation':-

Предоставля́ть в распоряже́ние; сдава́ть в эксплуата́цию	To put at someone's disposal; to put into commission

(10) The dependent noun denotes a process of cleaning, repair, etc.:-

Отдава́ть в почи́нку, в сти́рку, в кра́ску, в чи́стку	To put in for repair, for washing, dyeing, cleaning

(11) The dependent noun denotes waste materials:-

Кни́ги отправля́лись вути́ль	Books used to be sent for scrap
Сдава́ть в металлоло́м, в макулату́ру	To discard as scrap-metal, as scrap-paper

(12) The dependent noun denotes 'route', 'journey':-

Отправля́ться в путь, в кругосве́тное пла́вание	To set off on a journey, on a voyage round the world

В доро́гу combines with forms which denote not only 'departure', but also 'arrangements', 'preliminaries':-

Шли спе́шные сбо́ры в доро́гу	Hasty arrangements were being made for departure
Снаряжённая в доро́гу; оде́тый в доро́гу	Equipped for the road; dressed for the road
Ра́зве то́лько умы́ться, вот, в доро́гу	Maybe just wash before leaving

Some dependent nouns denote military operations:-

Пошёл в наступле́ние, в ата́ку	Went on to the offensive, into the attack

or 'pursuit', 'flight':-

Бро́сились в пого́ню	They rushed off in pursuit
Враги́ уда́рились в бе́гство	The enemy took to their heels

(13) The dependent noun denotes representatives of occupations, organisations, social groups, etc. (cf. в + locative 10 page 23) :-

Ма́льчики собира́ются в космона́в- ты	Boys have ambitions to be space- men
Брать в ночны́е сторожа́	To engage as a night watchman
Устро́иться в дво́рники	To get a job as a janitor
Быть произведённым в полко́вники	To be promoted to colonel
Приня́ть в пионе́ры	To accept into the Pioneers
Записа́ться в дружи́нники	To enlist as a voluntary militia- man
Зову́ в свиде́тели норве́жца	I call the Norwegian as witness

Приня́ть в чле́ны	To accept for membership
Вы́бран в депута́ты	Elected as a delegate
Вы́йти, вы́браться в лю́ди	To make one's way in the world
Идти́ в го́сти	To go visiting

Note constructions with годи́ться:-

Он не годи́тся в офице́ры	He is not cut out to be an officer

In the following, the construction expresses the meaning of relative age:-

Он годи́тся ей в отцы́	He is old enough to be her father
Она́ мне в до́чки годи́тся	She is young enough to be my daughter

Note The apparent nominative plural forms in this section are in fact relics of a former accusative form. The concept of plurality has now in many cases been lost, e.g.:-

Вы взя́ли себе́ в мужья́ феномена́льного обжо́ру	You have taken a phenomenal glutton as your husband

(14) Use of the preposition in time expressions:-

(a) the phrase answers the question во ско́лько (вре́мени)? (в кото́ром часу́?) 'at what time?':-

В час, в пять мину́т шесто́го, в че́тверть пя́того, в .по́лдень, по́лночь (but: в полови́не пя́того 'at half past four, без пяти́ пять 'at five to five')	At one o'clock, at five past five, at quarter past four, at midday, at midnight

(b) the phrase answers the question в како́й день? 'on what day?':-

Во вто́рник бы́ло партсобра́ние	There was a Party meeting on Tuesday
В э́ту, про́шлую, бу́дущую сре́ду	This, last, next Wednesday
Он поги́б в пе́рвый же день войны́ (for usage with ordinals above пе́рвый see на + accusative 25(a) page 61)	He was killed on the very first day of the war

This also applies to some plural forms (cf. по + dative 7, page 117):-

В бу́дни, в выходны́е дни, в обы́чные дни, в платёжные дни,	On weekdays, on days off, on normal days, pay days,

в пра́здники   on holidays

(c) the preposition combines with the names of parts of the day, when qualified by forms such as э́тот 'this', тот же 'the same', etc.:-

В ту ночь, в таку́ю ночь, в ночь перед полётом	That night, on such a night, on the night before the flight
В э́то у́тро; в у́тро, о кото́ром идёт речь	On this morning; on the morning in question
В э́тот ве́чер зацвели́ левко́и	On this evening the stock had bloomed
В тёплые ле́тние вечера́	On warm summer evenings
В бе́лые но́чи тури́сты прихо́дят сюда́ посмотре́ть на э́то чу́до	On the white nights the tourists come here to see this miracle

and with the names of seasons of the year when qualified other than by э́тот 'this', про́шлый, 'last', бу́дущий 'next':-

В то ле́то, в пе́рвую весну́	That summer, in the first spring
В го́рькую, тру́дную зи́му	In a bitter, difficult winter
Уны́ло во́ет ве́тер в дождли́вую холо́дную о́сень	The wind howls mournfully in a cold rainy autumn
В ту зи́му, в ту о́сень	That winter, that autumn

similarly with неде́ля 'week', ме́сяц 'month', год 'year', when qualified by пе́рвый 'first' or by adjectives denoting periods or seasons:-

В пе́рвые неде́ли о́сени выпада́ют иногда́ таки́е дожди́	Sometimes rain like this falls in the first weeks of autumn
Её муж пропа́л бе́з вести в пе́рвый ме́сяц войны́	Her husband went missing in the first month of the war
Мо́жно бу́дет освеща́ть Заполя́р-ные райо́ны в зи́мние ме́сяцы	It will be possible to illum-inate the Polar regions in the winter months
В дере́вню она́ верну́лась в пе́рвый год войны́	She returned to the village in the first year of the war
В послевое́нные го́ды	In the post-war years
В 20-е го́ды (also: в 20-х года́х)	In the twenties

(d) the preposition combines with 'general' time words:-

В а́томный век	In the atomic age
В сре́дние века́ европе́йские госуда́рства воева́ли из-за се́льди	In the Middle Ages European states fought over herring

Живём в историческое время	We live in historic times
В период между 1971–1975 годами	In the period between 1971 and 1975
Дома́ заселя́ли в разга́р весны́ (cf. рабо́та в по́лном разга́ре 'work is in full swing')	The new houses would be occupied at the height of spring
Де́лались в старину́ таки́е кора́лловые кре́стики	Coral crosses like that used to be made in the old days

Note: The compound preposition во вре́мя combines with the names of events: во вре́мя войны́ 'during the war', while в тече́ние usually combines with time words: в тече́ние десяти́ лет 'during the course of ten years'.

(e) the phrase answers the question в како́м во́зрасте? 'at what age'?:-

В пятна́дцать лет я получи́л пла́менное призна́ние в любви́	At the age of fifteen I received a passionate declaration of love

(f) the context indicates recurrence at regular intervals:-

Три ра́за в год, 150 рубле́й в ме́сяц	3 times a year, 150 roubles a month

(g) the dependent item denotes a climatic feature (cf. на + locative 7 page 50):-

Ни в дождь, ни в снег не уходи́ла соба́ка с аэродро́ма	The dog did not leave the aerodrome either in rain or snow
В плоху́ю пого́ду це́лые вечера́ проси́живал перед на́шим телеви́зором	In bad weather he would spend whole evenings in front of our television set
Истреби́тели в тума́н бы́ли прико́ваны к земле́	In the fog the fighters were grounded

other dependent items include:-

Ве́тер, гроза́, жара́, зной, моро́з(ы), нена́стье, речны́е полово́дья, пурга́, шторм	Wind, thunder-storm, heat, intense heat, frost, bad weather, river flooding, snow-storm, gale

(h) the prepositional phrase combines with a phrase in из, denoting continuity:-

Из ме́сяца в ме́сяц, из го́да в год	Month after month, year after year

(i) the prepositional phrase denotes the time taken to complete an action:-

Я реши́л вы́здороветь не в 5	I decided to recover not in five

ме́сяцев, а в 3	months, but in three

Cf. за + accusative 10(b) page 80). Note: only в appears in the following:-

В мгнове́ние о́ка, в одно́ мгнове́ние, в счи́танные мину́ты, в два счёта	In the twinkling of an eye, in an instant, in a few brief minutes, in two shakes
Сло́жные вопро́сы он реша́л в оди́н миг	He solved difficult problems in a flash

(j) the dependent noun denotes an event (cf. на + locative 10, page 51, where emphasis is rather on place):-

В войну́ пошёл доброво́льцем на фронт	In the war he volunteered for the front
Кто из молодёжи рабо́тал в вече́рнюю сме́ну?	Which of the young people worked on the evening shift?
В одну́ из таки́х бомбёжек бы́ло разру́шено крыло́ университе́та	A wing of the university was destroyed in one of these bombings

Note also: в отсу́тствие 'in the absence of' (cf. в прису́тствии 'in the presence of'. See в + locative 17, page 28).

(k) the preposition combines with раз qualified by an ordinal numeral:-

В пе́рвый раз	For the first time

(15) The dependent noun denotes the object:-

(a) of forms that indicate 'contact', 'collision', 'aim', etc.:-

Ты в меня́ поду́шкой бро́сил	You threw a pillow at me
Попа́сть ка́мнем в цель	To hit the target with a stone
Сде́лано мне три уко́ла: в о́бе руки́ и в живо́т	I have had three injections: in both arms and my stomach
Ра́нен в го́лову	Wounded in the head
Уда́р в че́люсть (but: уда́ры по, in reference to repeated or diffuse blows, cf. по + dative 9, page 118)	A punch on the jaw
Вы́стрелил в са́мую кру́пную ры́бу (but: стреля́ть по 'to fire on, at a diffuse, multiple target', cf. по + dative 9, page 118)	He fired at the largest fish

Other items include:-

Куса́ть в, лиза́ть в, стуча́ть в, целова́ть в	To bite on, to lick on, to knock at, to kiss on

(b) of forms that indicate 'playing':-

Играть в футбол, шахматы	To play football, chess
Играть в автомобиль, войну, в 'дочки-матери', лётчики, в кошки-мышки, отцы и матери, в сыщики и воры, свои соседи	To play cars, war, 'daughters and mothers', airmen, cat and mouse, fathers and moth- ers, cops and robbers, neighbours

Note: the 'orthodox' animate accusative plural is found in some combinations:- играть в 'индейцев', в космонавтов, to play 'Red Indians', spacemen.

Игра в блошки, городки, в жмурки, классы, в прятки, салки, снежки, в крестики и нолики, бабки	A game of tiddleywinks, gorodki, blind man's buff, hopscotch, hide and seek, tig, snowballs, noughts and crosses, knuckle- bones

(c) of forms that indicate 'belief':-

Верить, вера в бога	To believe, belief in God

(d) of the verb влюбляться 'to fall in love':-

Он влюбился в медсестру	He fell in love with a nurse

(16) The dependent noun denotes an aperture, optical aid, etc.:-

Я видел в окно освещённый солнцем двор	Through the window I saw the sun- lit yard
Я смотрю на себя в зеркало	I look at myself in the mirror
В бинокль рассматривает реку	Examines the river through bin- oculars

Other phrases include:-

В лупу, микроскоп, в окуляр, стереотрубу	Through a magnifying-glass, a microscope, an eye-piece, a periscope

Cf. a similar meaning in the following:-

Выкрикивал в рупор результаты	He was shouting out the results through a loud-hailer
Крикнуть в мегафон	To shout through a megaphone

(17) The prepositional phrase denotes manner, in terms of:-

(a) colour:-

Окрасить дом в яркий оранжевый цвет, в голубую краску	To paint a house bright orange, light blue

(b) design, pattern:-

Бума́га в кле́точку	Squared paper
Чулки́ в кра́сную и си́нюю поло́ску	Red and blue striped stockings
Ке́пка в кра́пинку	A spotted cap

(c) rhythm, tone, harmony:-

Его́ те́ло пульси́рует в такт му́зыке	His body pulsates in time to the music
Он в бе́лой руба́шке и га́лстуке в тон костю́му	He is in a white shirt and a tie to match his suit
Дви́гались они́ в лад, ро́вно дыша́	They moved in harmony, breathing evenly

(18) Meanings of extent and measure:-

(a) extent or measure is expressed in terms of real objects:-

Кабеля́ толщино́й в ру́ку	Cables the thickness of one's arm
Батаре́йка разме́ром в спи́чечный коробо́к	A battery the size of a match box
Улыба́ться во весь рот	To smile broadly

Note constructions with рост:-

Упа́л, вы́тянулся во весь рост	He fell, measured his full length

(b) extent or measure is expressed in abstract terms:-

Я́щики длино́й в 12 ме́тров	Boxes 12 metres long
Река́ глубино́й в три ме́тра	A river 3 metres deep
Доска́ толщино́й в 2 сантиме́тра	A board 2 centimetres thick
Бо́ксы пло́щадью в квадра́тный метр	Isolation compartments a square metre in area
Дви́гатель мо́щностью в 20 лошади́ных сил	A 20 horse-power engine
Гора́ высото́й в 2 500 ме́тров	A mountain 2,500 metres high

The following dimensions or measures also appear in the construction, often in the instrumental:- вес 'weight, объём 'volume, capacity', ра́диус 'radius', сто́имость 'value', ширина́ 'width'.

The name of the dimension may be omitted where no ambiguity is possible:-

Турби́на в 200 000 килова́тт	A 200,000 - kilowatt turbine
Места́ в три рубля́	3-rouble seats
Прыжо́к в ты́сячу ме́тров	A jump of 1,000 metres

Ток в 20 миллиампéр	A current of 20 milliamperes

Note also:-

Со скóростью в 30 киломéтров в час	At a speed of 30 kilometres per hour
Водоизмещéние в 4 000 тонн	A displacement of 4,000 tons
Температýра в 40 грáдусов	A temperature of 40 degrees

Note: в may be omitted in the type of construction described in section b (especially in the press, and in colloquial, scientific and technical registers), where a dimensional or mensural term is present in the construction:- сýдно грузоподъёмностью 11½ тысяч тонн 'a vessel with a freight-carrying capacity of 11,500 tons'.

(c) extent may also be expressed in terms of (i) component parts:-

Бумáжка в три строкú	A three-line message
Семьá в два человéка	A family of two

(ii) instalments:-

Открыть окнó в два движéния	To open a window in 2 movements
В одúн приём	At one go, at one sitting
Выпить стакáн в два приёма	To drain a glass in 2 draughts

(d) phrases which denote the intensity of scrutiny, listening, sound:-

Смóтрит во все глазá	He is all eyes
Во все ýши, в два ýха слýшает	He is all ears
Кричáть во всё гóрло, во весь гóлос, во весь рот	To shout at the top of one's voice

(e) set phrases in мочь, сúла:-

Напрягáться во всю мочь	To strain oneself to the limit
Светúть в пóлную сúлу	To shine with utmost intensity

(19) The prepositional phrase denotes the purpose of the dominant action:-

Мáрлон Брáндо выступил в защúту прав америкáнских индéйцев	Marlon Brando spoke up in defence of the rights of the American Indians
Я пóднял óбе рукú в знак примирéния	I raised both hands as a sign of reconciliation
Во избежáние этой двусмысленности развивáется нóвая констрýкция	A new construction develops in order to avoid this ambiguity

Боро́ться во и́мя побе́ды	To struggle in the name of victory
Магистра́ль сооружена́ в обхо́д Ми́нска	The main road has been built to by-pass Minsk
Он смея́лся в отве́т на их приве́тствие	He laughed in answer to their greeting
Монтевиде́о получи́л своё назва́ние в па́мять о ра́достном восклица́нии матро́са	Montevideo was named in memory of a sailor's cry of joy
А меня́ хоте́ли настро́ить в по́льзу одного́ подсуди́мого (cf. испо́льзовать что́-нибудь во вред челове́честву 'to use something to the detriment of mankind')	They wanted to prejudice me in favour of a certain defendant
Вы́двинуть предложе́ние в противове́с оппоне́нту	To put forward a proposal to counter one's opponent
Назва́ть сы́на в честь те́стя Алекса́ндром	To name one's son Alexander in honour of one's father-in-law
Анто́н в шу́тку называ́л То́ню тёзкой	For a joke Anton would call Tonya his namesake

Other phrases include:-

В доказа́тельство,	In proof,
в заключе́ние,	in conclusion,
в издёвку,	in ridicule,
в наказа́ние,	as a punishment,
в награ́ду,	as a reward,
в насме́шку,	in mockery,
в обме́н на,	in exchange for,
в ознаменова́ние,	to mark,
в отме́стку,	in revenge,
в подтвержде́ние,	in confirmation,
в по́мощь (кому́-н.),	as an aid to (someone),
в уго́ду (кому́-н.),	to please (someone),
в уще́рб (кому́-н./чему́-н.)	to the detriment of (someone/ something)

Note also the non-purposive: в доверше́ние всего́ 'to cap it all', 'to make matters worse'.

(20) Representative meanings. The dependent noun denotes:-

(a) 'debt', 'gift', 'legacy', etc.:-

Дава́ть, брать в долг 100 рубле́й	To lend, borrow 100 roubles
Дом я получи́л в насле́дство от	I received the house as a legacy

отца́	from my father
Получа́ть в пода́рок	To receive as a present
Дава́ть в зало́г, в зада́ток	To give as a pledge, as a deposit
(b) 'example', 'model':-	
Его́ ста́вили всем в приме́р	He was presented as an example to all

(21) The preposition combines with раз and multiples:-

В три ра́за то́лще, в полтора́ ра́за бо́льше	Three times thicker, half as much again

III

ИЗ + GENITIVE CASE

(1) The prepositional phrase denotes withdrawal from the types of location described in в + locative 1 (see pages 9-11):-

Он приéхал из гóрода	He has arrived from the town

в + locative 2 (see page 11):-

Выхóдить из автóбуса, лóдки, самолёта, троллéйбуса	To alight from a bus, a boat, a plane, a trolleybus

в + locative 5 (see pages 12-21, but cf. also c + genitive 3, pages 68-69):-

Переезжáть из москóвской квартúры в другóй гóрод	To move from a Moscow flat to another town
Бéгает из кýхни в столóвую	Runs from the kitchen to the dining-room
Слёзы брызнули у неё из глаз	Tears started from her eyes
-Это от той? - спросúла Зóя из дáльнего концá палáты	'Is that from her?', asked Zoya from the far end of the ward

The phrase also combines with phrases in в to denote continuity of movement:-

Из концá в конéц, из сторонь́ в стóрону, из углá в ýгол	From end to end, side to side, corner to corner
Писáтель Смирнóв éздил из гóрода в гóрод, из дерéвни в дерéвню в пóисках материáлов о герóях Отéчественной войнь́	The writer Smirnov went from town to town, from village to village in search of materials about the heroes of the Fatherland War

(2) The dependent noun may denote a state or condition (cf. в + locative 7, page 22):-

Решéние вь́рвать э́того человéка из безвéстности	The decision to bring this man out of obscurity
Возвращáться из óтпуска	To return from holiday

Вы́куп из крепостно́й нево́ли   Serf redemption

(3) The dominant form denotes one or more of a larger number of
items:-

Са́мый злове́щий из всех земны́х   The most sinister of all earthly
   зву́ков - ти́канье часо́в   sounds is the ticking of a clock

(4) The dependent noun denotes components:-

Со́лнце состои́т из водоро́да и   The sun consists of hydrogen and
   ге́лия   helium

Кома́нда из шести́ челове́к   A six-man team

(5) The dependent noun denotes source:-

Он шёл в костю́ме из гру́бого   He was walking in a suit made of
   сукна́   coarse cloth

Мо́жно экранизи́ровать рома́н и   One can screen the novel and make
   сде́лать из него́ фильм   a film out of it

Из рога́тки мо́жно стреля́ть   One can shoot stones from a cata-
камня́ми   pult

(6) The dependent noun denotes the motive of a deliberate action
(cf. от + genitive 4, page 95, which deals with the causes of
involuntary actions):-

Я собира́л ряби́ну из любви́ к   I was picking rowan-berries out
   э́тим воспомина́ниям о де́тстве   of affection for these childhood
                                   memories

Уби́йство из ре́вности   Murder for motives of jealousy

Он отказа́лся из упря́мства   He refused out of obstinacy

Солга́л из стра́ха   He lied out of fear

Other phrases indicating motivation include:-

Из ве́жливости, из жела́ния,   Out of politeness, out of a de-
из за́висти, из интере́са,   sire, out of envy, out of inter-
из любопы́тства, из нетерпе́ния,   est, out of curiosity, out of
из предосторо́жности, из   impatience, out of caution, out
   пренебреже́ния, из прили́чия,   of disdain, out of decency, on
из при́нципа, из тру́сости, из   principle, out of cowardice, out
   уваже́ния   of respect

(7) The prepositional phrase combines with a phrase in в + accusative to denote temporal continuity:-

Из ме́сяца в ме́сяц, из го́да в   Month after month, year after
   год   year

IV

HA + LOCATIVE/PREPOSITIONAL CASE

(1) The preposition's central meaning is 'on':-

На полу́, по́лке, столе́, на стене́, сту́ле	On the floor, shelf, table, wall, chair, etc.

Categories of dependent noun also include:-

(a) the names of certain buildings, structures, areas, organisations (cf. в + locative 1(a), page 9):-

На аэродро́ме, вокза́ле, на да́че, на дому́, на заво́де, ме́льнице, по́чте,	At the aerodrome, the main station, the villa, on the premises, at the factory, the mill, the post office,
на почта́мте, предприя́тии, на скла́де, ста́нции, на телегра́фе, фа́брике, на фе́рме	the main post office, the works, the warehouse, the station, the telegraph office, the factory, the farm
Он рабо́тает на скла́де	He works at the stores
Кро́ме трудодне́й Уткин зараба́тывает и на дому́	Apart from his work day units Utkin earns extra money at home

(b) the names of certain parts of dwellings and other structures (cf. в + locative 1(c)i, page 10):-

На ве́рхнем, ни́жнем этаже́	On the top, bottom floor
На тёмном чердаке́ висе́ли свя́зки ряби́ны	Bunches of rowan-berries hung in the dark attic

Note also usage with these parts of a ship:-

На корме́, носу́, па́лубе	In the stern, the prow, on the deck

(c) the names of certain sections in academic institutions (cf. в + locative 1(c)ii, page 10):-

На юриди́ческом факульте́те	In the law faculty
Я рабо́таю на ка́федре хи́мии	I work in the chemistry depart-

ment

| Учи́ться на филфа́ке | To study in the arts faculty |

(d) the names of certain sectors of theatrical accommodation (cf. в + locative 1(c)iv, page 10):-

| На балко́не, галёрке, я́русе | In the balcony, gallery, circle |

(e) the names of certain geographical features:-

(i) points of the compass:-

| На се́вере, ю́ге, восто́ке, за́паде | In the north, south, east, west |

| На Кра́йнем Се́вере, Да́льнем Восто́ке | In the Far North, Far East |

(ii) certain climatic zones and natural features:-

| На возвы́шенности, лугу́, на по́люсе, поля́не, на про́секе, равни́не, на целине́, эква́торе, | On high ground, on a meadow, at the Pole, in a glade, in a forest cutting, on a plain, on virgin soil, on the equator |

| На лугу́ пасло́сь ста́до коро́в | On the meadow grazed a herd of cows |

(iii) islands, peninsulas and archipelagoes (cf. в + locative, 1(d)iv, page 10):-

| На Аля́ске, Гава́йях, на Камча́тке, Кана́рах, Ки́пре, на Ко́льском полуо́строве, Кри́те, на Кури́лах, Ку́бе, Лабрадо́ре, на Ма́льте, Но́вой Гвине́е, на Сахали́не, Филиппи́нах, на Чуко́тке, Эльбе | In Alaska, the Hawaian Islands, Kamchatka, the Canaries, Cyprus, the Kola Peninsula, Crete, the Kuriles, Cuba, Labrador, Malta, New Guinea, Sakhalin, the Philippines, Chukotka, Elba |

| Наполео́н роди́лся на Ко́рсике | Napoleon was born in Corsica |

| На Ка́при с 1906 г. по 1913 г. жил М. Го́рький | M. Gorky lived on Capri from 1906 to 1913 |

| Са́мый се́верный вы́ступ Азии – мыс Челю́скин – нахо́дится на Таймы́ре | The most northerly promontory of Asia – Cape Chelyuskin – is in the Taimyr Peninsula |

(iv) mountain ranges and areas designated by a singular noun (cf. в + locative 1(d)v, pages 10-11):-

| На Алта́е, Кавка́зе, на Пами́ре, Тянь-Ша́не, Ура́ле | In the Altai, the Caucasus, the Pamirs, Tien Shan, Urals |

as well as some ranges with plural names:-

| На Балка́нах, Ле́нинских гора́х | In the Balkans, on Lenin Hills |

(v) the shores of seas, oceans, rivers, lakes:-

На Чёрном мо́ре, Ба́лтике, на Ка́спии, Во́лге, Днепре́,	On the Black Sea, the Baltic, the Caspian, the Volga, the Dnieper,
на Дуна́е, Куба́ни, Оби, на Байка́ле, Ми́чигане	the Danube, the Kuban', the Ob', Baikal, Lake Michigan
На Колыме́ добыва́ют ка́менный у́голь	Coal is mined on the Kolyma
Порт на Ти́хом океа́не	A port on the Pacific

(vi) the Ukraine and administrative regions ending in - щина:-

На Бря́нщине, Днепро́вщине, на Смоле́нщине, Ха́рьковщине	In Bryansk Region, Dnieper Region, Smolensk Region, Kharkov Region
На Украи́не дете́й ме́ньше, чем роди́телей	In the Ukraine there are less children than there are parents

(vii) the words ро́дина, чужби́на:-

На ро́дине; на чужби́не	In one's own country; in a foreign clime

and Русь:-

Екатери́на II ца́рствовала тогда́ на Руси́ (cf.: в дре́вней Руси́ 'in ancient Russia')	Catherine II was at that time on the throne in Russia

(viii) the names of certain city regions (cf. в + locative 1(d) viii, page 11):-

Теа́тр и́мени Вахта́нгова нахо́дится на Арба́те	The Vakhtangov Theatre is in Arbat
Большо́е строи́тельство разверну́лось на Со́коле и Октя́брьском по́ле	A major building project has been launched in Sokol and October Field
На Пре́сне	In Presnya

(ix) certain parts of a town (cf. в + locative 1(d)ix, page 11):-

На бульва́ре, мостово́й, на на́бережной, окра́ине, на перекрёстке, на пло́щади, проспе́кте, у́лице, на ры́нке	On the boulevard, roadway, embankment, outskirts, crossing, in the square, prospect, street, at a market

(f) words denoting places for sporting activity:-

На лы́жной ба́зе, на беговой доро́жке, на катке́, на ко́рте, на спорти́вной площа́дке, на стадио́не, на тре́ке	At the ski centre, the running track, the rink, on the court, at the sports ground, at the stadium, on the track
Он оди́н из са́мых авторите́тных рефери́ на ри́нге	He is one of the most authoritative referees in the ring

'Торпе́до' на своём по́ле проигра́ло арме́йцам Ленингра́да 2:6	'Torpedo' lost at home to the Leningrad army team 2:6

(g) the media, entertainment:-

Он рабо́тает на теа́тре, на ра́дио	He works at the theatre, on the radio (professional usage)
Не зна́ю, быва́ют ли на телеви́дении летучки	I do not know if they have emergency meetings at the TV studio

(h) names of meetings:-

Я был на прези́диуме, коми́ссии, комите́те	I was at a meeting of the presidium, the commission, the committee

(i) Planets, etc.:-

Температу́ра на Луне́ коле́блется в преде́лах $-160°$ до $+120°$	The temperature on the Moon fluctuates between $-160°$ and $+120°$
На Земле́, Со́лнце, Юпи́тере	On Earth, the Sun, Jupiter

(j) courses, lines of communication, etc.:-

На междугоро́дных ли́ниях — зелёные и́ли кра́сные авто́бусы	There are green or red buses on the inter-city routes
Пе́рвый ме́сяц на орби́те принёс и пе́рвый урожа́й с косми́ческого огоро́да	The first month in orbit also brought the first harvest from the market garden in space
Ве́ра на про́воде (cf. на друго́м конце́ про́вода 'on the other end of the line')	Vera is on the line
Радиогра́мма была́ передана́ на частоте́ 'и́грек'	The radiogram was transmitted on 'Y' frequency

(k) miscellaneous:-

Я отдыха́л на куро́рте	I holidayed at a spa
На сберкни́жке не оста́лось ни. рубля́	Not a single rouble remained in his savings book
То́нкая ни́точка на снегу́ вела́ на се́вер	The thin thread in the snow led north

Other phrases include the following:-

На де́реве,	In a tree,
на расстоя́нии, на ре́йде,	at a distance, in the roads (nautical),
на сковороде́, на друго́й стороне́,	in a frying pan, on the other side,

на всех у́ровнях   at all levels

(2) The dependent noun denotes a mode of transport. The dominant item normally denotes travelling (cf. в + locative 2):-

На авто́бусе, тролле́йбусе   On a bus, a trolleybus

Лю́ди всё вре́мя куда́-то е́дут   People are going somewhere all
  на поезда́х, самолётах,   the time on trains, aircraft,
  такси́, тролле́йбусах   taxis, trolleybuses

Две остано́вки на метро́ до   Two stops on the Underground to
  Арба́та   Arbat

Домо́й он верну́лся на трамва́е   He returned home on a tram

Прилете́л на вертолёте   He arrived in a helicopter

Ню́ре нра́вится е́здить на ли́фте   Nyura likes going in the lift

Note that the following appear only with на:-

На корабле́, парохо́де, су́дне   In a ship, steamer, vessel

(3) Dependent nouns which combine with either на or в. For a comparative survey, see в + locative (5, pages 12-21):-

(4) Meanings of support, foundation. The dependent noun denotes (a) physical support, foundation, in the form of:-

   (i) soles, heels:-

На каучу́ке, платфо́рме,   On rubber soles, platform soles,
  на то́лстой подмётке, ко́жаной   a thick sole, a leather sole,
  подо́шве, на микропо́рке   microcellular soles

Ту́фельки на высо́ком каблуке́   High-heeled court shoes

   (ii) fasteners:-

Бе́жевое пла́тье на кно́пках   A beige dress with fasteners

Но́сит сапоги́ на мо́лнии   He wears boots with zippers

Боти́нки на шнурка́х   Shoes with laces

   (iii) hinges:-

Дверь на пе́тлях   A door on hinges

   (iv) linings:-

Пиджа́к на ва́те; шу́ба на   A padded jacket; a coat lined with
  бе́личьем меху́   squirrel fur

Пальто́ на шёлковой подкла́дке   A coat with a silk lining

   (v) other types of physical base or support, attachment, etc.:-

Ката́ться на конька́х; ходи́ть на   To skate; to ski
  лы́жах

Рука́ на пе́ревязи   An arm in a sling

Матрац на пружинах	A mattress on springs

Other phrases include:-

На костылях, на привязи, на якоре	On crutches, on a lead, at anchor

(b) the basis of diet, food, etc.:-

(i) dietary contexts:-

Он воспитывался на жирном крестьянском молоке	He was raised on thick peasant milk
Мы целую неделю просидели на одной селёдке	We lived just on herring for a whole week

Note also:-

Быть, держать, сидеть на диете, кефире, тюремном пайке, хлебных карточках	To be, to keep, to exist on a diet, kefir, prison rations, bread coupons

(ii) culinary base:-

Готовить на маргарине, сале, жарить на масле	To cook in margarine, lard, to fry in oil
Варенье на сахаре, патоке	Jam made with sugar, syrup

(iii) the base for infusion, flavouring of drinks:-

Настаивать водку на лимоне, вишне	To prepare vodka with lemons, cherries

(iv) medicinal contexts:-

Он жил на морфии и камфаре	He was on morphine and camphor

(c) the dependent noun denotes a source of power:-

Приёмник работал на сухих батареях	The receiver worked on dry batteries
Стереосистемы на транзисторах	Stereo systems operating on transistors
Завод работает на нефти	The factory operates on oil

(d) moral basis:-

Меня воспитывали на разных положительных примерах	I was reared on various positive examples
Учиться на примерах	To learn by example

(e) legal basis:-

На правах бывшего мужа выпрашивает эту льготу	He applies for this privilege on the basis of his rights as a former husband
На этих условиях	On these terms

(5) The dependent noun denotes types of state and condition:-

Находи́ться на иждиве́нии, находи́ться на пе́нсии, быть на попече́нии, состоя́ть на слу́жбе	To be maintained, to be on a pension, to be in care, to be in service
Она́ была́ уже́ на преде́ле своего́ терпе́ния	She was at the end of her tether
Тео́рию на пра́ктике на́до перевари́ть	Theory must be assimilated in practice
Ты заключённый. Кем был на во́ле? (also: на свобо́де 'at liberty')	You are a convict. What was your job outside?

(6) The dependent noun denotes a stage in a process:-

На пе́рвой ста́дии	At the first stage
Каки́м бы примити́вным ни́ был язы́к на пе́рвых эта́пах	However primitive language may have been in its early stages

Dependent nouns may indicate stages in more specific terms:-

На 4-м витке́ косми́ческий кора́бль пролете́л над Мадри́дом	On its fourth circuit the space ship passed over Madrid
Па́ртия заверши́лась на 16-м ходу́	The game ended at the 16th move
Стре́лка замерла́ на нуле́	The pointer stopped at zero
На 136-м киломе́тре попере́к шоссе́ стоя́л полоса́тый шлагба́ум	At the 136th kilometre a striped barrier barred the highway

(7) Climatic conditions (cf. в + accusative 14(g), page 35 for a temporal variant):-

На ле́тнем со́лнце, на ветру́ загоре́л он почти́ до черноты́	He burned almost black in the summer sun and the wind
Облива́ться по́том на жаре́	To sweat gallons in the heat
Валуны́, кото́рые на лю́том моро́зе обжига́ли ру́ки	Boulders which scorched the hands in the severe frost
Он рабо́тает почти́ на косми́ческом хо́лоде	He is working in the almost cosmic cold

(8) The dependent noun denotes language, dialect, etc.:-

Говоря́т они́ на 120 языка́х	They speak 120 languages
Сказа́ла э́то на чи́стом пари́жском наре́чии	She said it in pure Parisian dialect

Other dependent nouns include диале́кт, жарго́н.

(9) The dependent noun denotes an object by means of which an action is accomplished:-

Игра́ть на скри́пке, фле́йте	To play the violin, the flute
Печа́тать на маши́нке, размножа́ть на маши́нке	To type, to duplicate
На парашю́тах мо́жно спуска́ться весьма́ прице́льно	One can parachute on to a target with extreme precision

The dominant item may denote a financial operation:-

Ско́лько де́нег мо́жно сде́лать на их прода́же?	How much can be made on their sale?
На зарпла́те эконо́мится о́коло 1м. рубле́й	About 1m. roubles is saved on salaries

Dominant items also include:-

Де́лать при́быль, надува́ть, нажива́ться	To make a profit, to cheat, to make a fortune

(10) The dependent noun denotes an event:-

На бале́те, на вы́борах, на кани́кулах, на похорона́х, на охо́те, на приёме, на рабо́те, на сва́дьбе, на съе́зде ...	At the ballet, elections, in the holidays, at a funeral, a hunt, a reception, at work, at a wedding, a congress ...
На сме́не, пока́ бе́гаю по эстака́де, ка́к-то забыва́ется боль	At the shift, as I run about on the gantry, the pain is somehow forgotten
Она́ провали́лась на экза́менах	She failed the examinations
Психоло́гия челове́ка на войне́	The psychology of people at war

(11) The dependent noun denotes 'speed', 'gear':-

И я на по́лной (большо́й, преде́льной) ско́рости перехожу́ с пе́рвой доро́жки на втору́ю	I switch from the first to the second lane at full (high, maximum) speed
Я завёл свою́ маши́ну и на тре́тьей ско́рости въе́хал в село́	I started my car and drove into the village in third gear
Вы е́дете на четвёртой переда́че	You are driving in fourth gear
Стара́йтесь всё вре́мя держа́ть автомоби́ль на переда́че	Try to keep the car in gear all the time
Езда́ на 'нейтра́ли' не эконо́мит то́пливо	Driving in neutral does not save fuel

(12) The phrase на де́ле, на са́мом де́ле, in contrastive use:-

-На вид таки́е ми́лые, а на са́мом де́ле злы́е	-Seemingly so nice, but in fact spiteful
Но на де́ле он был безоби́дным мужичко́м	But in fact he was an inoffensive fellow

and in confirmatory use (cf. в + locative 16, page 28):-

Где собира́ется хоть два одесси́та - там уже́ ве́село. И на са́мом де́ле весёлая у нас была́ разведро́та	Where even two Odessans gather the atmosphere is cheerful. And indeed, we had a very happy recce company

(13) Expressions of time. The dependent nouns include:-

Век (meaning 'lifetime'):-

Быва́лые морепла́ватели повида́ли на своём веку́ мно́гие стра́ны	Experienced seafarers have seen many countries in their time

Неде́ля

На э́той, про́шлой, бу́дущей неде́ле	This week, last week, next week

Па́мять

На мое́й па́мяти Москва́ соверше́нно преобразова́лась	Within my memory Moscow has been completely transformed

Рассве́т (зака́т, заря́)

Он верну́лся на рассве́те	He returned at dawn

Ста́рость лет

На ста́рости лет чаепи́тие заменя́ет ей чуть ли не все удово́льствия	In her old age tea-drinking is a substitute for virtually all her pleasures

as well as time expressions which denote a stage in a process:-

Он на 76-м году́ потеря́л зре́ние	He went blind in his 76th year
Она́ сообщи́ла, на како́м ме́сяце бере́менности он оста́вил её	She informed us in which month of her pregnancy he had abandoned her
На 6-й мину́те сове́тские хоккеи́сты открыва́ют счёт	In the 6th minute the Soviet hockey team opens the score

(14) The dependent noun or phrase denotes the object of items indicating (a) marrying:-

Он жени́лся в 1928-м году́ на хоро́шенькой блонди́нке	He married a pretty blonde in 1928
Его́ жени́тьба на Джозефи́не	His marriage to Josephine

  (b) concentration, specialisation, etc.:-

Вся эне́ргия сосредото́чивается на том, что́бы попа́сть в цель	His whole energy is concentrated on hitting the target

Other items include:-

Заде́рживать внима́ние на, специализи́роваться на	To keep one's attention on, to specialise in

(c) effect:-

Боле́знь сказа́лась на его́ похо́дке	His illness showed in his walk
Это хорошо́ отрази́лось на его́ здоро́вье	It was good for his health

(d) operation or experimentation:-

На заключённых испы́тывали но́вые ядови́тые вещества́	They tested new poisonous substances on the prisoners
За опера́цию на пе́чени беру́т ты́сячу до́лларов	They charge a thousand dollars for an operation on the liver

(e) irritation, spite:-

Вымеща́ть зло́бу, доса́ду на ко́м-нибудь	To vent one's spite, vexation on someone
Почему́-то и́менно на нём сорва́л зло́бу генера́л	For some reason the general vented his spleen on him

(f) insistence:-

Наста́ивать на встре́че, на приня́тии мер	To insist on a meeting, on measures being taken

(15) The dependent noun denotes heart, mind, conscience:-

На душе́ кака́я-то тя́жесть	Something is weighing on my mind
Тоска́ лежи́т на се́рдце	His heart is weighed down with melancholy
Вина́ лежи́т на мое́й со́вести	Guilt weighs on my conscience

V

HA + ACCUSATIVE CASE

(1) The dominant form indicates motion on to or to a location.
For the types of location involved see на + locative 1, page 44)
:-

Он поста́вил таре́лку на стол	He put the plate on the table
Она́ пове́сила карти́ну на́ стену	She hung the picture on the wall

Categories of dependent noun also include the names of certain
buildings, etc. (cf. на + locative 1(a), page 44):-

На вокза́л, да́чу,	To the main station, the villa,
на заво́д, по́чту,	the factory, the post office,
на телегра́ф, фе́рму	the telegraph office, the farm

of certain parts of buildings (cf. на + locative 1(b), page 44):-

Лезть на черда́к	To climb into the attic
Подня́ться на шесто́й эта́ж	To go up to the fifth floor

of certain sections of academic institutions (cf. на + locative
1(c), pages 44-45):-

На ка́федру, факульте́т	To the department, faculty

of certain sectors of theatrical accommodation (cf. на + locative
1(d), page 45):-

На галёрку	To the gallery

of certain geographical features (mountains, ranges, islands,
peninsulas, city regions, etc. (cf. на + locative 1(e), pages 45-
46):-

На Кавка́з, Камча́тку, Ку́бу, на Куба́нь, ро́дину, Ура́л	To the Caucasus, Kamchatka, Cuba, the Kuban', the homeland, the Urals
Соверша́ть подъём на Казбе́к, на Памѝр, Алта́й	To make an ascent of the Kazbek, the Pamirs, the Altai
На окра́ину, ры́нок, на у́лицу	To the outskirts, the market, the street

Подвезла́ пассажи́ров на Арба́т   I drove some passengers to Arbat

(2) The dependent noun denotes a means of transport (cf. на + locative 2, page 48):-

Сади́ться на авто́бус, по́езд,   To board a bus, a train,
на самолёт, такси́, трамва́й,   a plane, a taxi, a tram,
на тролле́йбус, сади́ться на   a trolleybus, to mount a bicycle
велосипе́д

(3) A number of dependent nouns combine with either в or на + accusative (see в + accusative 4, pages 29-30):-

(4) The prepositional phrase combines with particular dominant items which imply direction:-

Биле́т на о́перу (but: биле́т в   A ticket for the opera
теа́тр)

Вид на весь го́род   A view of the whole town

Вторже́ние на чужу́ю террито́рию   Invasion of someone else's ter-
(but: вторже́ние в Аме́рику)   ritory

(5) The dependent noun denotes means of support, attachment, basis, etc. (cf. на + locative 4, pages 48-49):-

Парохо́д стал на я́корь   The steamer hove to

Она́ посади́ла соба́ку на́ цепь   She put the dog on a chain

Налега́ть на костыли́   To bear down on one's crutches

Сажа́ть на хлеб и на́ воду   To put on bread and water

(6) The dependent noun denotes types of state and condition (cf. на + locative 5, page 50):-

Он вы́пустил пти́цу на во́лю   He set the bird free

Поступи́л на вое́нную слу́жбу   He enlisted for military service

Выходи́ть на пе́нсию   To go on the pension

(7) Meanings of general direction and orientation:-

(a) the dependent noun denotes or implies a final destination:-

Доро́га на Берли́н   The road to Berlin

Расписа́ние самолётов на Ново-   The schedule of aircraft for
сиби́рск и Челя́бинск   Novosibirsk and Chelyabinsk

a visible orientation point:-

Ехать на костёр   To ride in the direction of the
    bonfire

or a sound:-

Двигаться на голос	To move in the direction of the voice

(b) the dominant form denotes a gesture or other signal:-

Кивнул на сверток в моих руках	He nodded at the bundle in my hands
Никто на детей не цыкал	No one shut the children up

Other forms include повышать голос на 'to raise one's voice to', топать ногой на 'to stamp one's foot at', шикать на 'to shush at'

(c) the dominant form denotes various types of verbal and written comment:-

Стихи на смерть А. Толстого	Verses on the death of A. Tolstoy
Рецензия на книгу	A review of a book

Other items include:-

Доносить на, жаловаться на, заявлять на, клеветать на	To denounce, to complain of, to report (someone), to slander

(8) The dominant form denotes projection over a distance:-

Передача электричества на тысячи километров	The transmission of electricity over thousands of kilometres
Сосна простирается на 150 км.	The pines extend for 150 kilometres
Толкнул ядро на 20 метров	He put the shot 20 metres
Бег на 5000 метров	The 5,000 metres race

(9) The dominant item may also denote sonic projection:-

Кричит на весь двор	He shouts loudly enough to be heard all over the yard
Диктор на всю страну объявил, что отбит Ростов	The announcer proclaimed for all the country to hear that Rostov had been recaptured

In a variant of this construction, the dominant item denotes fame:-

Слава на весь мир	World-wide fame
На весь свет прославленный советский цирк	The world-famous Soviet circus

(10) The dependent noun denotes an event (cf. на + locative 10, page 51):-

Уеду на встречу с американской делегацией	I shall leave for a meeting with the American delegation
Ушёл на войну	He went off to the war

Выбежали на тренировку	They ran out to train
Поезд отправляется в Омск на годовой ремонт	The train sets out for its annual overhaul in Omsk

(11) The dominant item denotes a feeling of vexation, offence, etc.:-

Я тайла на отца много обид	I nursed many grudges against my father
Негодуя на неё за молчаливый отказ от приглашения	Indignant with her for her silent rejection of the invitation
Он был зол на меня	He was angry with me

Other items include:-

Гнев на, досада на, обижаться на, раздосадованный на, сердиться на	Anger with, vexation with, to take offence at, vexed with, to get angry with

(12) The dominant item denotes determination to take certain action:-

Идти на компромисс, идти на сделку, идти на риск, идти на уступки	To resort to a compromise, to make a bargain, to take a risk, to make concessions
Он идёт на лишения	He accepts privations
Институт пойдёт на любые расходы	The institute will go to any expense
Мало кто решается на такой выбор	Few decide on such a choice
Как он мог бы отважиться на такое поистине великое дело?	How could he have ventured on such a truly great cause?
Он готов на всё,	He is prepared to go to any lengths,
готов на любую дерзость,	prepared to perpetrate any insolence,
готов на любые жертвы,	prepared for any sacrifice,
готов на любое унижение	prepared to endure any humiliation
Он способен на более длительное испытание	He is capable of a more protracted ordeal

(13) The dominant item denotes expenditure (a) of effort:-

Виктор все силы направил на подготовку к выборам	Victor directed all his efforts towards preparation for the election

Other dominant items include отдавать свои силы на 'to devote one's energies to'.

(b) of time:-

Трáтить врéмя на чтó-нибудь	To spend time on something

(c) of money:-

Трáтить дéньги на пустякú	To spend money on trifles
Правúтельство вы́делило на развúтие городскóго хозя́йства Москвы́ два миллиáрда рублéй	The government allocated 2,000,000,000 roubles for the development of the municipal economy of Moscow

Note also the implication of expenditure in the following:-

Копúть на пальтó; зарабáтывать на жизнь	To save up for a coat; earn one's living
Дéньги на дорóгу, на текýщие расхóды	Money for travelling expenses, for current expenses.

(14) Meanings of allocation, designation, etc.:-

Кóмната на двоúх	A double room
Мост, рассчúтанный на 15 тонн	A bridge designed to carry 15 tons
Лес на пострóйку; материáл на ромáн; матéрия на костю́м; мех на шýбу; отрéз на плáтье	Timber for building; material for a novel; material for a suit; fur for a coat; a dress length

Note the meaning of designation in the context of meals and menus:-

Что на обéд, на пéрвое, на закýску?	What is for lunch, for first course, for hors d'oeuvres?

(15) The dependent noun denotes the object of study

(a) the dependent noun denotes the name of a profession:-

Учúться на инженéра	To study to be an engineer

(b) the dominant item denotes testing:-

Экзáмен на получéние водúтельских прав	Driving test
Кóнкурс на млáдшего наýчного сотрýдника	A competition for junior scientific assistant

(c) the dominant item denotes a piece of work:-

Диссертáция на стéпень кандидáта технúческих наýк	A dissertation for the degree of kandidat in technical sciences

(16) The dependent noun denotes the purpose or object of testing :-

Проводúла испытáния нóвого шлéма	She was testing the new helmet

на про́чность	for toughness
Проверя́ет семена́ на схо́жесть	She checks the seeds for germinating capacity
Про́ба на совмести́мость кро́ви	A blood compatibility test
Разве́дка на нефть	Prospecting for oil

Other items include иссле́довать на 'to examine for'

The dominant item may denote competition:- ма́тчи на ку́бок Дэ́виса 'Davis Cup matches'

Note a figurative use:-

Олимпиа́да - э́то прове́рка на му́жество, мастерство́ и сто́йкость	The Olympics are a test of courage, skill and determination

(17) The dominant phrase denotes a precaution (constructions with слу́чай):-

Спусти́лся в овра́г, на вся́кий слу́чай с ножо́м в руке́	He descended into the gully with a knife in his hand, just to be on the safe side
Ложи́лся полуоде́тым (на слу́чай бомбёжки)	He would go to bed half-dressed (in case of a bombing raid)
Назвала́ своё и́мя на слу́чай, е́сли им ещё когда́-нибудь доведётся встре́титься	She gave her name, just in case they should ever chance to meet again

(18) The dominant item denotes work performed for the benefit of the dependent item:-

Оди́н рабо́тал на всю семью́	He worked unaided for the whole family
Стира́ла и што́пала на всю семью́	She washed and darned for the whole family

Note the figurative variants:-

Труди́ться на бла́го ми́ра; вре́мя рабо́тает на него́	To work for the good of the world; time is on his side

(19) The dominant item denotes encouragement, coercion:-

Па́ртия наце́ливает наро́д на ускоренное разви́тие земледе́лия	The Party directs the people towards an accelerated development of agriculture
Подбива́ть на демонстра́ции	To incite to demonstrations
Подгова́ривать на сде́лку	To instigate a deal

(20) The dominant item denotes permission or authorisation:-

Разрешéние на въезд	Entry permit
Заключи́ть договóр на сценáрий	To conclude a contract for a script
Удостоверéние на прáво вождéния	A driving licence
Наря́д на погрýзку	A warrant for loading
Кáрточки на бензи́н	Petrol coupons
Рецéпт на таблéтки	A prescription for tablets
Талóн на обéд	A meal voucher

Other items include:-

Óрдер на, уполномóчивать (на ведéние дéла)	Requisition for, to empower (to transact some business)

The dominant item may also denote a sound or other signal:-

Давáть комáнду на начáло рабóты; звонóк на урóк; давáть 'добрó' на чтó-либо	To give the order to start work; the lesson bell; to give the go-ahead for something

(21) The dominant item denotes submission to a process denoted by the dependent item:-

Он отпрáвил проéкт в Москвý на утверждéние	He sent the project to Moscow for confirmation
Онá сдалá емý чемодáн на хранéние	She handed the suitcase into his safe keeping
Онá принеслá емý докумéнты на пóдпись	She brought him the documents for signature
Брать ребёнка на воспитáние; брать на порýки; вноси́ть бумáги на обсуж-дéние; направля́ть дéло на расслéдо-вание	To adopt a child; to go bail for; to introduce papers for discussion; to submit a case for investigation

(22) Meanings associated with departure, retiring, etc.:-

Он кивнýл на прощáние головóй	He nodded his head in farewell
Бухáнка хлéба на дорóгу	A loaf of bread for the journey
На сон грядýщий совершáл прогýлку	He would go for a walk before retiring

(23) Constructions with годи́ться (the dependent form is often a pronoun of the type что, чтó-нибудь, etc.):-

Футболи́сты теря́ют фóрму и ни на чтó не годя́тся	Footballers lose their form and are no good for anything

Всё в жизни на что́-нибудь   Everything in life is some good
   годи́тся

(24) The dominant item denotes division, breaking-up, etc., while
the dependent items denote (a) the result of disintegration:-

Разруби́ть шкаф на ще́пки   To hack a cupboard to pieces

   (b) objects which are utilisable:-

Коло́ть дере́вья на дрова́   To chop trees for firewood

Рвать бельё на тря́пки   To tear up linen for rags

   (c) objects obtained by cannibalisation:-

Разобра́ть телеви́зоры на дета́ли, To dismantle TV sets for the
   маши́ну на запасны́е ча́сти   parts, a car for the spare parts

Note also constructions with разделя́ть:-

Верхо́вный Сове́т СССР разделён   The Supreme Soviet of the USSR
   на две пала́ты   is divided into two chambers

and cf.:-

Умножа́ть це́лое число́ на дробь   To multiply a whole number by a
                                 fraction

(25) Temporal meanings. Dependent items denote:-

   (a) time segments qualified by a numeral above пе́рвый (cf. в +
accusative 14(c), page 34) or by сле́дующий:-

Хорони́ли его́ на сле́дующий   They buried him on the next day
   день

Ли́па зацвета́ет на 72-й   The lime tree flowers on the 72nd
   день   day

Вы́ход в откры́тый ко́смос на   A walk in space on the 172nd day
   172-е су́тки полёта   of the flight

На сле́дующий ве́чер, на   The next evening, the next
   сле́дующее ле́то, на   summer, the next night
   сле́дующую ночь

На тре́тье у́тро он откры́л   On the third morning he opened
   глаза́   his eyes

На втору́ю неде́лю отва́лится   In the second week one of the
   кака́я-нибудь из но́жек   legs will fall off

На второ́й год в учи́лище мы   In our second year in the academy
   ста́ли устра́ивать свои́   we began to organise our own
   вечера́   parties

   (b) the names of certain festivals:-

На па́сху, рождество́, тро́ицу   At Easter, Christmas, Whitsun

Compare also the association with a celebration in:-

Дари́ть приёмник на сва́дьбу	To give a radio for a wedding present

(c) a time for which something is arranged or designated:-

Собра́ние назна́чено на седьмо́е ма́рта	A meeting has been arranged for March 7
Уро́к на за́втра	Tomorrow's homework

(d) the time which follows the completion of an action:-

Он на́ год пое́хал за грани́цу	He went abroad for a year
Пря́тала на́ лето зи́мние ве́щи	She would put her winter things away for the summer
Сего́дня он встал с посте́ли на 5 мину́т и опя́ть лёг	Today he got up for five minutes and then went back to bed

(e) a date which pin-points a particular night:-

Это была́ ночь с 11-го на 12-е января́	It was the night of January 11-12

(f) the phrase на э́тот раз:-

На э́тот раз не челове́к охо́тился за зве́рем, а зверь охо́тился за челове́ком (also в э́тот раз)	This time it was not a man hunting an animal, but an animal hunting a man

(26) Determinative meanings. The prepositional phrase (a) localises the dominant item (usually an adjective):-

О́стрый на у́хо, о́стрый на язы́к	Sharp eared, sharp tongued
Хромо́й на пра́вую но́гу, глухо́й на о́ба у́ха, слепо́й на ле́вый глаз	Lame in the right leg, deaf in both ears, blind in the left eye

(b) defines the object of the dominant item:-

Мо́да на старину́	A fashion for antiques
Не уплати́л нало́га на соба́ку	He has not paid his dog licence
Спрос на сове́тские малолитра́жки	The demand for Soviet mini-cars
Це́ны на вторсырьё	The prices of secondary raw materials
Зака́з на пла́тье	An order for a dress
Пра́во на о́тдых	The right to relaxation
Разгово́р на интере́сную те́му	A conversation on an interesting subject

(27) Meanings of extent and quantification (a) of a physical action:-

Подтянул ремень на две дырочки   He tightened his belt two holes

(b) in terms of percentages and fractions:-

Земля на три четверти океан   The Earth is 3/4 ocean

Выполнять норму на 105%   To fulfil one's norm by 105%

(c) in terms of a difference, expressed by comparatives or other-wise:-

Он на три года старше меня   He is 3 years older than me

Население увеличилось на 1   The population increased by a
миллион   million

(d) in terms of monetary value:-

Штрафовать на 5 рублей   To fine five roubles

Страховка на 10 000 долларов   Insurance for 10,000 dollars

На рубль марок   A rouble's worth of stamps

Чек на 10 000 рублей   A cheque for 10,000 roubles

(e) in terms of scholastic achievement:-

Учиться на круглые пятёрки   To get straight A's

Сдать экзамены на четвёрки   To get 'very good' in the exams

Писать сочинение на 'отлично'   To get 'excellent' for one's
                                   essay

(f) in terms of ratio:-

Единственный хирург на весь   The only surgeon in the whole
район   region

Добиться того, чтобы на каждые   To arrange for there to be two
три квартиры было два   telephones to every three flats
телефона

(g) in terms of phrases expressing 'to the full extent':-

Включить приёмник на полную   To turn the radio up full
мощность

Пустить отопление на полный   To turn the heating full on
ход

Other examples include:-

Работать на всю мощность,   To work to full capacity, to
пустить душ на полную силу   turn the shower full on, etc.

(28) Constructions which denote means of accomplishment, in terms of (a) the senses:-

На глаз больные растения ничём   To the eye, sick plants in no
не отличаются от здоровых   way differ from healthy ones

На слух я подбирал модные в ту   I could pick out the then fash-

пору мелодии | ionable tunes by ear

(b) locking devices:-

Пирамиды с оружием заперты на замки́ | The pyramids of weapons are secured with locks

Закрыва́ть на ключ, на засо́в | To lock, to bolt

(c) money:-

Купи́ть на два рубля́ | To buy for 2 roubles

Идти́ в кино́ на его́ счёт я не мог | I could not go to the cinema at his expense

На таки́е де́ньги он мог ме́сяц пита́ться | With that kind of money he could feed himself for a month

Жить на зарпла́ту, прира́боток, на сбереже́ния, стипе́ндию | To live on one's salary, additional earnings, savings, a scholarship

(d) fishing gear:-

Рыба́лка на одну́ у́дочку | Fishing with one rod

(29) Meanings of similarity:-

Они́ о́чень похо́жи друг на дру́га | They are very much alike

Он сма́хивал на каку́ю-то пти́цу | He resembled some kind of bird

Я вы́гляжу на 30 лет | I look 30

Other items include the verb походи́ть на 'to resemble'. Note also the set phrases:-

Это на него́ похо́же!; это ни на что́ не похо́же! | That's just like him!; I've never seen anything like it!

(30) Meanings of basis (a) in musical contexts:-

Пе́сня 'Огро́мное не́бо' на слова́ Рожде́нственского | The song 'The Vast Sky' to the words of Rozhdestvensky

(b) in contexts of trust and responsibility:-

Ве́рить на́ слово | To take someone's word

Я на свою́ отве́тственность стал всем писа́ть 'дорога́я' или 'дорого́й' | On my own responsibility I began to address everyone as 'dear'

(31) Phrases of manner:-

Жить на широ́кую но́гу | To live in the grand style

Он карта́вит на францу́зский мане́р | He has a guttural pronunciation, in the French manner

Стихи́ мо́жно писа́ть то́лько на | One can write poems only on

голодный желудок	an empty stomach
Она называла Сашу на 'ты'	She addressed Sasha as 'thou'
Расчёсанные на пробор седины	Grey hair combed with a parting
Езда на красный цвет	Jumping the lights
На новый лад; на свой лад	In the new manner; in one's own way
Поставлены были на подобие скамей длинные ящики из-под яиц	Long egg-boxes had been placed in the manner of benches

(32) The prepositional phrase denotes the object of a verb or other form:-

И на меня произвёл скверное впечатление	He made a bad impression on me too
Мы охотились на уток	We were hunting ducks (i.e. 'to hunt to kill'. Cf. охота, охотиться за 'to hunt to catch'. See за + instrumental 3)
Покушаться на самоубийство; покушаться на чью-либо жизнь	To attempt suicide; make an attempt on someone's life
Посягать на чью-либо свободу, чьё-либо имущество	To encroach on someone's liberty, property

Other items include:-

Влиять на; надеяться на;	To influence; to rely on, hope for;
обращать внимание на; оказывать влияние на; оказывать давление на; рассчитывать на; соглашаться на	to pay attention to; to exert influence on; to exert pressure on; to count on; to agree to

(33) Meanings of reaction:-

Ответ на, в ответ на письмо,	An answer to, in answer to a letter,
отвечать на письмо	to answer a letter
Откликаться на призыв	To respond to an appeal

Other items include:-

Реагировать на, реакция на, отзываться на	To react to, reaction to, to respond to

(34) The dependent noun denotes a climatic feature (cf. на + locative 7, page 50):-

Выскочить на обжигающий мороз	To leap out into the searing frost
Вылезать из мешка на холод и дождь	To climb out of a sleeping bag into the cold and rain

(35) Meanings of transfer:-

Обменивать старьё на игрушки	To exchange old clothes for toys
Переводить на русский	To translate into Russian (cf. на + locative 8, pages 50-51)
Переходить на низшую передачу	To change down (to a lower gear) (compare на + locative 11, page 51)

(36) Meanings of purpose:-

Выпьем на брудершафт	Let's drink to fraternity
Играть на деньги	To play for money
На память о нашей встрече	In memory of our meeting
Очередь на новую квартиру	A queue for a new flat
Двух дней нам хватит на эту поездку	Two days are all we need for this journey
На пари	For a bet

(37) Miscellaneous:-

Повезло Надюшке и на мужа	Nadyushka was also lucky in her husband
Всем на смех подхватил воспаление лёгких	To everyone's amusement he caught pneumonia

VI

C + GENITIVE CASE

(1) In its central meaning the preposition denotes withdrawal from the types of location dealt with in на + locative 1, pages 44-48, including certain buildings and areas, parts of buildings and institutions, geographical features, etc.:-

С по́ла, по́лки, со сту́ла	From the floor, the shelf, the chair
С вокза́ла, заво́да, с куро́рта, со стадио́на, со ста́нции	From the main station, the factory, the spa, the stadium, the station
С аэродро́ма он е́хал в пусто́м авто́бусе	He was riding from the aerodrome in an empty bus
С галёрки	From the gallery
Она́ вы́прыгнула со второ́го этажа́	She jumped from the first floor
Он с юриди́ческого факульте́та	He is from the law faculty
С Кавка́за, Ура́ла	From the Caucasus, the Urals
С се́вера, ю́га, восто́ка, за́пада	From the north, south, east, west
С Вене́ры, Земли́, Ма́рса	From Venus, Earth, Mars
Прибыва́ть с Ки́пра, Аля́ски	To arrive from Cyprus, Alaska
Я с Арба́та	I am from Arbat
Я получи́л письмо́ с ро́дины	I received a letter from home
С у́лицы никто́ бо́льше в рестора́н не рва́лся	No one was rushing in off the street into the restaurant any more
Съёмка с орби́ты в тече́ние пяти́ мину́т	Filming from orbit for the space of five minutes

(2) The dependent item denotes a vehicle. Cf. на + locative

(2, page 48) and из + genitive (1, page 42):-

С поезда на перрон сошёл молодой человек	A young man alighted from the train on to the platform

(3) The prepositional phrase represents the 'opposite' of the types of phrase in на + locative described in the contrastive survey which appears in в + locative (5):-

Не двинулся с места (cf. стоять на месте 'to stand still')	He did not move from the spot
Без гола он уходил с поля редко (cf. на футбольном поле 'on the football field')	He rarely left the field without scoring a goal
Домой он приходил с телестудии обычно ночью (cf. на телестудии 'at the TV studio')	He usually returned home from the TV studio at night
Собрался прыгнуть с 5-метровой высоты (cf. на высоте пяти метров 'at a height of five metres')	He made ready to leap from a height of five metres

Note that many phrases in с + genitive predominate over из despite the в/на dichotomy described in в + locative (5), thus:-

Самолёт с воздуха заметил терпящих бедствие (cf. самолёт в воздухе)	The aircraft spotted the victims of the disaster from the air
Не мог подняться с постели (cf. лежит в постели)	He could not get up out of bed
Пересекал весь посёлок, с горы и в гору (where с горы appears as the opposite of в гору)	He traversed the whole settlement, both downhill and uphill

According to Vsevolodova: 95, the following phrases in с are usually preferred to their counterparts in из:-

Со двора, с кровати, с неба, с огорода, с поля	From the yard, from bed, from the sky, from the market garden, from the field

Both prepositions appear to be possible with конец:-

Он спросил из/с дальнего конца палаты	He asked from the far end of the ward

С seems to be preferred with кресло, though both prepositions are found:-

Он встал с/из кресла	He got up from an armchair

С is commonly found with море:-

Он возвращался с мо́ря; с мо́ря пришёл звук	He would return from the sea; a sound carried from the sea, etc.

Note also:-

Демобилизова́лся с фло́та	He was demobilised from the navy

and uses with глаза́

Из глаз её хлы́нули слёзы	Tears welled from her eyes
Пото́м ты ладо́нью утёр слёзы с мои́х глаз	Then you wiped the tears from my eyes with the palm of your hand

(4) The preposition is common in spatial meaning when the dependent noun is qualified by весь:-

Посы́пались телегра́ммы – чуть ли не со всего́ све́та	The telegrams flooded in - virtually from all over the world
Ребя́та сбега́лись со всего́ го́рода	The lads were converging from all over the town
Со всей Норве́гии соберу́тся	They will gather from all over Norway

Other phrases include:-

Со всей Евро́пы, со всего́ ми́ра, со всей страны́	From all over Europe, from all over the world, all over the country

Note also the plural examples:-

Певцы́ прие́хали со всех концо́в Ла́твии	The singers came from every part of Latvia
Скве́рик со всех сторо́н окружён дома́ми	The small public garden is surrounded on all sides by houses

(5) The prepositional phrase combines with phrases in на + accusative to denote continuity of movement:-

С де́рева на де́рево, с ме́ста на ме́сто	From tree to tree, place to place,
Он вороча́лся с бо́ку на́ бок	He tossed from side to side

(6) The dependent noun denotes climatic conditions (cf. на + locative 7, page 50):-

Она́ вошла́ с моро́за	She came in out of the frost

(7) The dependent noun denotes an event or activity (cf. на + locative 10, page 51):-

С войны́, конце́рта, с конфере́нции, рабо́ты	From the war, a concert, a conference, work

| Он возвращался не со смены, не с вечеринки, а от приятеля | He was returning not from a shift, not from a party, but from a friend's house |

(8) The prepositional phrase denotes source:-

| Перевод с латинского (cf. на + locative 8 pages 50 -51 and на + accusative 35, page 66) | A translation from Latin |
| Рисовать с натуры; читать музыку с нот; снимать копию с оригинала | To draw from life; to sight-read (music); to take a copy from an original |

(9) The dominant item denotes exaction of a due:-

Я получала алименты с первого мужа	I was getting alimony from my first husband
Берёт с владельца пошлину	He exacts duty from the owner
Собирать налог с частников	To collect the tax from private owners
Сколько с меня?	How much do I owe you?

Other dominant items include:- брать дань 'to exact tribute', взимать пошлину 'to exact duty', взыскивать налог 'to exact a tax'.

Compare also figurative usage:-

| Какой спрос с мужчины? | What can you expect of a man? |

(10) The preposition's central temporal meaning is 'since', 'from'. The preposition combines:-

(a) with the names of time segments:-

| С субботы мы вместе | Since Saturday we have been together |
| С апреля будущего года Венгрия перейдёт на так называемое летнее время | As from April next year Hungary will switch to so-called summer time |

(b) with general time words, enabling the preposition to combine indirectly with the name of an event:-

Два десятилетия прошло со времени победы	Two decades have passed since the victory
Со дня новоселья	Since the house-warming
С момента получения вашего письма	Since the receipt of your letter

Note combinations with пора:-

С тех пор	Since then

Мы встречались уже полгода – с тех пор, как она прибыла в наш полк

We had been meeting for 6 months – since she had arrived in our regiment

С некоторых пор я понял, что с девчонками нечего церемониться

For some time I had realised there was no point in standing on ceremony with girls

(c) with nouns denoting stages in life:-

С детства, с юности — Since childhood, since my youth

(d) with words denoting the earlier of two terminal points in time:-

С 26 марта до 1 апреля

From March 26 to April 1 (March 31 is the last full day)

С 26 марта по 1 апреля

From March 26 to April 1 (April 1 is the last full day)

(e) the prepositional phrase combines with phrases in на + accusative to denote temporal immediacy:-

Он должен позвонить с минуты на минуту

He should ring any minute now

Other phrases include:-

Со дня на день, с часу на час — Any day now, any hour now

(11) Meanings of commencement, where (a) the dominant item denotes 'beginning':-

Их дружба началась с драки

Their friendship began with a fight

Он начал с того, что изображал ноги верблюда в 'Демоне'

He began by playing the legs of a camel in 'Demon'

Note the phrase: вставать с левой ноги:-

Встал сегодня с левой ноги

He got out of bed the wrong side today

(b) the context involves the spelling of initial letters:-

Писать с большой (заглавной, прописной) буквы, с малой буквы

To write with a capital letter, with a small letter

(c) the dependent item denotes the successful stage in a series :-

С первого же удара дверь открылась

The door opened at the very first blow

Со второй спички прикурил папиросу

He lit his cigarette with the second match

Самолёт лишь с трётьей попытки сумёл поднятьься в вёздух	Only at the 3rd attempt did the aircraft manage to take off
Алька поняла с пёрвого взгляда	Al'ka realised this at first glance

(12) Meanings of permission:-

С одобрёния, позволёния, с согласия	With the approval of, the permission of, the consent of
Приезжайте ещё – тóлько с разрешёния родителей	Come again – but with your parents' permission

(13) Meanings of cause. The dependent noun may denote a feeling :-

Плакать с гóря, со страха	To weep with sorrow, with fear
Вскрикивать с испуга	To cry out with fright
Горёть со стыда	To burn with shame
Краснёть с досады	To grow red with vexation

a physical sensation or state:-

Умирать с гóлоду	To starve to death
С похмёлья мрачный	Morose due to a hangover
Закоченёл с усталости	He grew stiff with fatigue

a natural phenomenon:-

Плясать со стужи	To jump up and down from the freezing cold

Note. The preposition от (see от + genitive 4) appears in a far wider range of expressions than с in denoting the cause of involuntary reaction or state, and may be regarded as the norm for this type of meaning. Some grammarians relate expressions with с to the colloquial register.

С is often found in figurative expressions:-

Умирать с досады, умирать сó смеху, умирать со скуки, с тоски	To die of vexation, to die laughing, to die of boredom, of melancholy, etc.

and appears in a number of set phrases:-

С жиру беситься	To become too fastidious
Ни с тогó ни с сегó	For no particular reason
С бухты-барахты решать вопрóс нет смысла	There is no point in deciding the question off the cuff
С какóй стати он отправился в самое пёкло?	For what reason did he plunge right into the thick of it?

Note also the phrase с непривычки 'due to lack of practice', etc.

VII

ЗА + INSTRUMENTAL CASE

(1) The preposition's central meaning is 'behind', 'on the other side of':-

За бóртом, зá гóродом, за грани́цей, за прилáвком, за рекóй, за рулём	Overboard, in the country (out of town), abroad, behind the counter, beyond the river, at the wheel
Температýра за бóртом самолёта былá -30°	The temperature outside the aircraft was -30°
Стари́к плáкал за двéрью	The old man was weeping outside the door
Дождь барабáнил за окнóм	The rain was pelting down outside the window
Их бы́ло чéтверо за столóм	There were 4 of them at the table
Он ждал за углóм	He was waiting round the corner

Note the figurative uses:-

Вот там, за углóм, счáстье; счáстье не за горáми	Happiness is there, just round the corner; happiness is at hand

and the prepositional adverb зáмужем:-

Онá зáмужем за рýсским	She is married to a Russian

The prepositional phrase combines with исчезáть, скрывáться:-

'Москви́ч' исчéз за поворóтом	The 'Moskvich' disappeared round the bend.

The preposition combines with the names of meals:-

За зáвтраком он старáлся её развлéчь	At breakfast he tried to amuse her

and the names of certain activities:-

Проводи́ть вéчер за игрóй; заставáть когó-нибудь за	To spend the evening playing; to find, catch someone reading

чте́нием

(2) The preposition denotes meanings of successiveness (a) in space:-

Самолёты взлете́ли оди́н за други́м	The aircraft took off one after another

 (b) in time:

Год за го́дом, день за днём	Year after year, day after day

(3) The dependent noun may denote the object of pursuit:-

Он охо́тился за перепела́ми	He was hunting quails

Other forms include:-

Бе́гать,бежа́ть за; гоня́ться,гнать-ся за; пого́ня за; сле́довать за	To run after; to chase; pursuit of; to follow

Note that гоня́ться, гна́ться and пого́ня appear in figurative contexts:-

Гна́ться за ли́чной коры́стью, за дли́нным рублём	To chase after personal gain, to make a fast buck
Пого́ня за при́былью, уда́чей	The pursuit of profit, success

The dependent noun may also denote the object of supervision, observation, etc.:-

Ко́шка с интере́сом наблюда́ла за соба́кой	The cat observed the dog with interest
Он следи́л за разви́тием те́хники	He followed the development of technology
Он уха́живает за ружьём	He looks after his gun

Other items include:-

Наблюде́ние за, присма́тривать за, смотре́ть за, ухо́д за	Observation of, to supervise, to look after, maintenance of

Some verbs in the series mean 'to woo, court':-

Капита́н уха́живает за ней	The captain is courting her

Other verbs meaning 'to woo' include волочи́ться, увива́ться.

(4) The dependent noun denotes the object of fetching, acquiring, etc.:-

Эти лётчики обеща́ли залете́ть за мной через не́сколько дней	These pilots promised to call for me in a few days' time
Он протяну́л ру́ку за деньга́ми	He stretched out his hand for the money
Очередь за водо́й	A queue for water

Note usage with the verb огля́дываться:-

Он огля́дывался за партнёрами	He was looking round for partners

and in abstract contexts:-

Он пришёл к ней за сове́том и по́мощью	He came to her for advice and help
Она́ подняла́ глаза́ на отца́, обраща́ясь к нему́ за подде́ржкой	She looked up at her father, appealing to him for support

(5) The prepositional phrase may denote (a) physical cause:-

За стено́й не ви́дно	You can see nothing for the wall
За шу́мом никто́ не слы́шал их разгово́ра	Nobody heard their conversation for the noise

(b) abstract cause, the dependent noun denoting absence:-

Лаборато́рия не рабо́тает за неиме́нием лабора́нта	In the absence of a laboratory assistant the laboratory is not functioning
Его́ оправда́ли за отсу́тствием ули́к	He was acquitted for lack of evidence

or non-serviceability, uselessness:-

Про́дали за нена́добностью	They sold it as not wanted
Бро́сить за него́дностью	To discard as worthless

(6) The dominant form denotes reservation, acknowledgement, etc., both (a) physical:-

Заче́м держа́ть за ним ко́йку?	Why keep a bed for him?
Опя́ть сло́во бы́ло за ним	It was his turn to speak again
За тобо́й о́чередь	It is your turn
Кни́ги чи́слятся за ва́ми	The books are out in your name
Сохране́ние за же́нщиной за́работка и ме́ста рабо́ты	Retention of a woman's salary and job

(b) abstract:-

За америка́нцами был приорите́т	The Americans enjoyed priority
Признаю́ пра́во за ка́ждым худо́жником на со́бственное прочте́ние кла́ссики	I acknowledge the right of every artist to his own reading of the classics
Гла́вное преда́тельство я оставля́ю за собо́й	I reserve the main treachery for myself

The meaning may indicate the presence of certain habits, behaviour:-

Он не замеча́л за ней	He did not detect any sentiment-

сентимента́льности	ality in her character
Я знал за ним э́ту привы́чку	I knew he had this habit
Призна́ет за собо́й часть вины́	He will acknowledge a part of the blame
За мной нет никако́й вины́	I am blameless

(7) The dependent noun denotes exception: вы́чет, исключе́ние:-

Литерату́ра - за немно́гим исключе́нием - воспева́ет самоотве́рженность матери	Literature - with minor exceptions - extols a mother's selflessness

VIII

ЗА + ACCUSATIVE CASE

(1) The preposition's central meaning is 'movement behind, beyond', etc. cf. за + instrumental case (1, pages 73-74):-

За границу, за дверь, за поворот, за реку, за руль	Abroad, outside the door, round the bend, over the river, at the wheel
Поехали за город на дачу	They drove into the country to the villa
Закладываю руки за голову	I place my hands behind my head
Я уселся за круглый стол	I took my place at the round table
Машина заехала за угол	The car turned the corner
За борт смыло повара	The cook was washed overboard

Note the prepositional adverb замуж:-

Дала слово выйти за него замуж	She promised to marry him

(2) The prepositional phrase may denote distance from a point:-

За 5 километров отсюда, в деревне Соболёвка, сегодня свадьба	Five kilometres from here, in the village of Sobolevka, there is a wedding today

Compare в + locative case (11, page 23). За is preferred (a) in combination with the preposition до:-

За 500 метров до финиша подтянулся англичанин	Five hundred metres from the finish the Englishman began to gain ground

(b) in combination with дверь, дом, квартал:-

За два дома от этого угла в 20-е годы было общежитие	In the 1920's there was a hostel two doors from this corner

(c) when the dominant item denotes movement to a goal:-

После работы она бежала за 8	After work she ran 8 kilometres

киломе́тров домо́й	home

(3) The preposition is used in constructions which denote excess :-

Моро́з уже́ за 30	There are already over 30° of frost
Бы́ло за́ полночь	It was past midnight
Ему́ за́ сорок	He is over forty
Давле́ние в бассе́йне перевали́ло за 100 атмосфе́р	The pressure in the pool exceeded 100 atmospheres

(4) The dominant verb denotes contact, seizure, etc.:-

Брать(ся) за, держа́ть(ся) за, дёргать за, задева́ть за, лови́ть за, обнима́ть за,	To take by, to hold by, to tug by, to brush against, to catch by, to embrace by, round,
поддёрживать за, привя́зывать за,	to support by, to attach by,
сти́скивать за, тро́гать за, трясти́ за, тяну́ть за, щипа́ть за	to squeeze by (on), to touch on, to shake by, to pull by, to pinch on
Он ведёт велосипе́д за руль	He is pushing the bicycle by the handlebars
Я взял И́нку за́ руку	I took Inka by the hand
Он схвати́лся за́ голову	He clutched his head
Спусково́й крючо́к зацепи́лся за край его́ оде́жды	The trigger caught on the hem of his clothing
Они́ шли держа́сь за́ руки	They walked hand in hand

Note a figurative variant:-

Он взя́лся (принялся́) за осуществле́ние пла́на	He set to work on the implementation of his plan

(5) The dependent noun denotes persons on whose behalf, instead of whom, actions and processes are carried out:-

За меня́ ду́мал Петро́в	Petrov thought for me
Она́ хо́чет, чтобы реши́ли за неё!	She wants them to decide for her!
Рабо́чие дава́ли обяза́тельство рабо́тать за двои́х	The workers pledged themselves to work enough for two

Other items include:-

Дежу́рить за, распи́сываться за	To be on duty in place of (to stand in for), to sign a receipt for

Note also:-

Отвечать за кого-нибудь, что-нибудь	To be responsible for someone, something

The dominant verb may denote intercession, advocacy:-

Агитировать за кандидата	To campaign on behalf of a candidate
Можно проголосовать за решение	One can vote for the decision
Молятся за упокой его души	They pray for the repose of his soul

Other items include:-

Заступаться за, ручаться за, хлопотать за, ходатайствовать за	To intercede for, to vouch for, to plead for, to petition for

The dependent noun may denote persons on whose behalf feelings are experienced:-

Она была оскорблена за него	She was offended on his behalf
Я рад за тебя	I am glad for you
Она боится за меня	She is afraid for me
Отцу за меня краснеть не пришлось	My father did not have to blush for me

Other items include:-

Волноваться за, гордость за, огорчён за, радоваться за, страх за, счастлив за	To be worried for, pride in, upset for, to rejoice for, fear for, happy for

(6) The dependent noun denotes the object of struggle, competition:-

Бороться за социализм	To fight for socialism
Соревноваться за высокие урожаи	To compete for high-yield harvests

Note also the phrase гибнуть за родину 'to die for the fatherland'.

(7) The prepositional phrase denotes 'in return for':-

Платить пришлось только за сахар	We only had to pay for the sugar
Батон за 28 копеек	A long loaf for 28 kopecks
Счёт за газ и электричество	The gas and electricity bill
Продавать за наличный расчёт	To sell for cash

(8) The dependent noun denotes the cause of thanks, reward,

blame, etc.:-

Спаси́бо за сове́т!	Thanks for the advice!
Меда́ль за отва́гу	A medal for bravery
Его́ суди́ли за кра́жу	He was tried for theft
Его́ наказа́ли за оши́бку	He was punished for his mistake

Other items include:-

Благодари́ть за, мстить за (дру́га), награжда́ть за, осужда́ть за, презира́ть за, приговаривать за, прославля́ть за, руга́ть за, уважа́ть за, хвали́ть за	To thank for, to avenge (a friend), to reward for, to condemn for, to despise for, to sentence for, to glorify for, to scold for, to respect for, to praise for

(9) The dependent noun denotes the object of evaluation, identification:-

Принима́ли её за мою́ де́вушку	They took her for my girl friend
Он вы́дал себя́ за специали́ста	He passed himself off as an expert
Он слывёт за знатока́	He is said to be a connoisseur

Other dominant items include сходи́ть за 'to be taken for'.

(10) Temporal meanings: (a) the prepositional phrase denotes the time during which an event occurs or events occur:-

Он встреча́л за э́то вре́мя не бо́лее 60 други́х автомоби́лей	During this period he encountered no more than 60 other cars
За де́сять лет то́лько два ра́за в теа́тре была́!	In ten years she has been to the theatre only twice!

Note the set phrase за после́днее вре́мя:-

За после́днее вре́мя повзросле́л	He has matured recently

(b) the phrase denotes the time taken to complete an action:-

За э́ти два го́да она́ из де́вочки преврати́лась в де́вушку	In these two years she was transformed from a girl into a young woman

Compare в + accusative (14(i), pages 35-36). Where the time appears excessive in relation to the task accomplished, за is normally preferred:-

В электросва́рке и за полго́да не разберёшься	You won't master arc-welding even in six months

(c) the phrase denotes the time by which one event precedes another:-

Пе́рвая радиогра́мма была́ принята́	The first radiogram was received

за час до полу́ночи   an hour before midnight

За час до вы́лета   An hour before take-off

(d) the phrase may denote the day or date of a publication:-

Возьми́ журна́л 'Мета́лл' за   Take the journal 'Metal' for
янва́рь-март э́того го́да   January-March of this year

(11) The phrase что за in the meaning како́й has no effect on the
case of the dependent noun:-

Что за му́ка!   What torment!

Что это за друзья́, е́сли мы   What kind of friends are we if we
бро́сим тебя́ в беде́?   leave you in the lurch?

IX

ИЗ-ЗА + GENITIVE CASE

(1) The preposition's central meaning is 'from behind', etc. cf.
за + instrumental (1) and за + accusative (1):-

Из-за двéри, окнá,	From outside the door, window,
из-за рекú,	from the other side of the river,
из-за руля́	from behind the wheel
Онá встáла из-за столá	She got up from the table
Из-за углá вы́шел какóй-то пáрень	Some chap came round the corner
Он вернýлся из-за грани́цы	He returned from abroad

(2) The dependent noun denotes external cause, in terms of objects, persons, or natural phenomena:-

Парохóд был лишён возмóжности маневри́ровать из-за огрóмной бáржи	The steamer was unable to manoeuvre because of an enormous barge
Из-за тебя́ все неприя́тности	All this trouble is because of you
Вспы́шки не так я́рки из-за дождя́	The flashes are less bright because of the rain

in terms of qualities, feelings, states, etc.:-

Лифт не рабóтает из-за обéденного переры́ва	The lift is not working because of the lunch break
Из-за невнимáтельности лаборáнта былá допýщена оши́бка в вычислéниях (cf. по + dative 12(d), where the feelings, qualities which constitute the cause are the subject's own)	A mistake was made in the calculations due to the inattentiveness of the laboratory assistant
Гóнка вооружéний продолжáется из-за стрáха обéих сторóн	The arms race continues because of the fear of both sides

X

ПОД + INSTRUMENTAL CASE

(1) The preposition's central meaning is 'under(neath):-

Мы стоя́ли под мосто́м	We were standing under the bridge

Note usage with the dependent nouns гора́, дождь, потоло́к:-

Он уви́дел её под горо́й	He saw her at the bottom of the hill
Ночь провели́ под дождём	They spent the night in the rain
Ла́мпы висе́ли под потолко́м	The lamps hung from the ceiling

in the set phrases:-

По́д боком, по́д носом, под руко́й	Near by, close at hand

in conjunction with the names of towns:-

Он уча́ствовал в боя́х под Москво́й	He took part in the battles near Moscow

in conjunction with the noun у́гол (in the meaning 'angle'):-

Улица выходи́ла под угло́м к трамва́йной остано́вке	The street came out at an angle to the tram stop

in conjunction with the names of crops under cultivation:-

По́ле под пшени́цей, ро́жью	A field under wheat, rye

in conjunction with verbs that denote comprehension:-

Что вы понима́ете под э́тим сло́вом?	What do you understand by this word?

(2) The dependent noun denotes physical and concrete state:-

Под аре́стом, под замко́м (под ключо́м), под но́шей, под обстре́лом, под пара́ми, под фла́гом	Under arrest, under lock and key, under a burden, under bombardment, under steam, under a flag
Под ружьём нахо́дятся о́коло	About five million men and of-

пятй миллибнов солдат и офицеров	ficers are under arms

and abstract state:-

Под бременем,	Under a burden (figurative),
под влиянием, под вопросом,	under the influence of, under discussion,
под командой, под контролем,	under the command of, under control,
под наблюдением, под надзором,	under observation, under supervision,
под давлением, под натиском,	under pressure, under the onslaught,
под опекой, под подозрением,	under the guardianship of, under suspicion,
под покровительством, под предлбгом,	under the patronage of, under the pretext,
под присмотром, под присягой, под стражей, под судом, под тяжестью	under supervision, under oath, under guard, on trial, under the weight of
Дом находится под охраной областного музея	The house is under the protection of the provincial museum
Эксперименты проводятся под руководством крупных учёных	The experiments are carried out under the guidance of leading scientists
Под действием ультрафиолетовых лучей кислород ионизируется	Oxygen ionizes under the effect of ultra-violet rays

XI

ПОД + ACCUSATIVE CASE

(1) The preposition's central meaning is 'movement to a position under, underneath' (cf. под + instrumental 1, page 83):-

Они́ се́ли под де́рево ста́ли под наве́с	They sat down under a tree, stood under an awning

Он спря́тал ру́ки под стол   He hid his hands under the table

Note usage with гора́, дождь:-

Спуска́ться под го́ру   To go downhill

Мы попа́ли под си́льный дождь   We got caught in heavy rain

usage in conjunction with the names of towns:-

Мы перее́хали под Ленингра́д   We moved to near Leningrad

and in agricultural and horticultural contexts:-

Обрабо́тать по́ле под капу́сту   To put a field under cabbage

(2) The dependent phrase denotes state or condition. (Cf. под + instrumental (2, pages 83-84):-

Брать под контро́ль;
  брать под наблюде́ние,
  под опе́ку,
  под подозре́ние, под стра́жу;
  отдава́ть под власть,
  под надзо́р;
  отдава́ть под суд;
  попада́ть под аре́ст;
  призыва́ть под ружье́;
  принима́ть под своё
  покрови́тельство;
  ста́вить под угро́зу
	To take control of,
	to place under observation,
	under the guardianship of,
	under suspicion, under guard;
	to place under the authority of,
	under supervision;
	to prosecute;
	to be placed under arrest;
	to call to arms;
	to take under one's patronage;
	
	to place under a threat

Журавлёв берёт меня́ под защи́ту   Zhuravlev takes me under his wing

(3) The preposition combines with ло́коть, мы́шки (armpits), рука́ in contexts of support:-

Они́ прогу́ливаются по́д руку	They are strolling about arm in arm
Его́ поддёрживали по́д руки	They were supporting him by the arms
Кого́-то из ро́дственников, недово́льных пригово́ром, вы́ведут под ло́кти на у́лицу	One of the relatives, who are dissatisfied with the verdict, will be frog-marched out on to the street

(4) The dominant verbs denote allocation or adaptation of an area for a particular function:-

Да́ли зе́млю под огоро́ды	They allocated land for market gardens
Ко́мнаты, отведённые под музе́й	Rooms, ear-marked as a museum

Other items include:-

Забира́ть под, приспоса́бливать под	To appropriate for, to adapt as

Some constructions involve containers and content:-

Отведена́ под ру́кописи старомо́дная корзи́на	An old-fashioned basket has been allocated for manuscripts

(5) The dependent noun denotes accompaniment:-

Ста́ли танцева́ть под старомо́дные фокстро́ты	They began to dance to the accompaniment of old-fashioned fox-trots

Other phrases include:-

Под аккомпанеме́нт, под аплодисме́нты, под орке́стр	To the accompaniment of, to applause, to an orchestra

Note also:-

Писа́ть под чью́-то дикто́вку	To write to someone's dictation

(6) In temporal meaning, the preposition denotes 'towards, approaching':-

Он верну́лся по́д вечер домо́й	He returned home towards evening
Встать под у́тро	To get up in the early hours

Other dependent nouns include:-

Коне́ц, ста́рость	End, old age.

In the context of holidays, the preposition means 'on the eve of' :-

Под Но́вый год, в ночь под Пе́рвое ма́я	On New Year's Eve, on May Day eve

Под выходно́й день я всегда́ уезжа́ю за́ город	I always go out of town on the eve of my day off
Под больши́е пра́здники на око́шко кла́ли ломо́ть хле́ба и́ли пиро́г	On the eve of great festivals they would place a slice of bread or a pie on the window-sill

The dependent noun may be an age in years:-

Ему́ под со́рок лет	He is getting on for forty

(7) Meanings of adaptation, assimilation in style, appearance, etc.:

Он запе́л под Шаля́пина	He began to sing in imitation of Shalyapin
Они́ бы́ли загримиро́ваны под кита́йцев	They were made up as Chinamen
Комо́д под кра́сное де́рево	An imitation mahogany sideboard
Подде́лка под же́мчуг	Fake pearls

The dependent noun may denote a hair style:-

Стри́чься под би́тлсов, стри́чься под ма́льчика	To have a Beatles cut, to have one's hair cut like a boy's

Short hair styles may be expressed in various ways:-

Стри́чься под бо́брик, под бо́кс, под гребёнку, под нулёвку	To have one's hair cropped, crew-cut, etc.

Note the figurative expression:-

Стричь под одну́ гребёнку	To reduce everyone to the same level

(8) The prepositional phrase denotes the basis of certain transactions:-

(a) financial ('against a pledge or other security'):-

Вы́брался из полице́йского уча́стка под зало́г в 5 000 до́лларов	I was released from the police station on security of $5,000
При́няли под квита́нцию де́ньги	They accepted the money against a receipt

(b) relating to responsibility:-

Андре́й реши́л отпра́вить брига́ду под свою́ отве́тственность	Andrei decided to dispatch the workteam on his own responsibility

XII

ИЗ-ПОД + GENITIVE CASE

(1) The preposition's central meaning is 'from under(neath)':-

Он спас де́вочку из-под по́езда	He saved a little girl from under a train

Note usage with the names of towns:-

Из-под Росто́ва	From near Rostov

(2) The prepositional phrase denotes withdrawal from various states (cf. под + instrumental case 2, pages 83-84 and под + accusative case, 2, page 85.

Освободи́ть из-под стра́жи	To release from custody
Маши́ны вы́йдут из-под контро́ля	The cars will get out of control
Выходи́ть из-под влия́ния	To escape from someone's influence
Он не мо́жет по́лностью вы́рваться из-под её вла́сти	He cannot entirely break loose from her authority

Note the figurative expression:-

Рабо́тать из-под па́лки	To work under compulsion

(3) The dependent noun indicates the former content of a container:-

Балло́н из-под га́за	A gas-cylinder
Ба́нка из-под варе́нья	A jam-jar

XIII

У + GENITIVE CASE

(1) The preposition's central meaning is 'at, by, near':-

У са́мой две́ри; у окна́	Right by the door; by the window
Слу́шала, сто́я у стола́	She listened, standing by the table

Note the figurative usage in:-

Стоя́ть у вла́сти	To be in power

(2) The prepositional phrase means 'at the house of', etc.:-

Она́ отдыха́ет у сестры́ в дере́вне	She is staying with her sister in the country
Вчера́ Са́ша был у врача́	Yesterday Sasha was at the doctor's
У нас есть по́лная за́нятость	In our country there is full employment

(3) Possessive meanings:-

У меня́ своя́ маши́на; у меня́ нет маши́ны	I have my own car; I haven't got a car

The prepositional phrase can function as a possessive:-

Ру́ки у нёе дрожа́ли	Her hands were shaking
Прове́рено зре́ние бо́лее чем у 200 000 шко́льников	The eyesight of more than 200,000 school-children has been tested

(4) The dependent noun denotes the source of buying, borrowing, etc.:-

Я купи́л дом у дя́ди	I bought the house from my uncle
Он занима́ет у них де́ньги	He borrows money from them
Я беру́ у него́ уро́ки лати́нского	I take Latin lessons from him

Я попроси́л у него́ каранда́ш	I asked him for a pencil
Спроси́те доро́гу у милиционе́ра	Ask a policeman the way
Я мно́гому научи́лся у э́того па́рня	I learnt a lot from this fellow

Other items include:-

Арендова́ть у, выи́грывать у, красть у, лечи́ться у,	To lease from, to win from, to steal from, to take treatment from,
отнима́ть у, снима́ть у, узнава́ть у (also узнава́ть от)	to take away from, to rent from, to find out from

XIV

K + DATIVE CASE

(1) The preposition's central meaning is 'towards':-

Я побежа́л к вы́ходу	I ran towards the exit

The preposition also appears in phrases denoting stance:-

Стоя́ли бо́ком к мосту́	They stood sideways on to the bridge
Мы стоя́ли лицо́м друг к дру́гу	We stood face to face

The dependent noun may be animate:-

Больно́й пошёл к врачу́	The patient went to see the doctor
Визи́т Наде́жды к Сая́новым	Nadezhda's visit to the Sayanovs
Обраща́ться с вопро́сом к кому́-нибудь	To address a question to someone

The dependent noun may denote an action or an abstract idea:-

Попы́тка к бе́гству	An attempt at escape
Путь к сча́стью	The path to happiness
Стремле́ние к вла́сти	Ambition for power
Сре́дства к жи́зни	Means of livelihood

(2) The dominant form denotes coercion, appeal, indication, etc. :-

Принужда́ть ко лжи	To force into prevarication
Не могли́ склони́ть Джорда́но Бру́но к отка́зу от свои́х иде́й	They could not persuade Giordano Bruno to renounce his ideas
Подава́ть сигна́л к ата́ке	To give the signal for attack
Звоно́к к у́жину	The supper bell

Other items include:-

Побужда́ть к, подстрека́ть к, призыва́ть к (поря́дку)	To induce to, to incite to, to call to (order)

(3) The dominant form denotes an accompanying part, component or supplement:-

Начи́нка к пирогу́	Filling for a pie
Увертю́ра к 'Пи́ковой да́ме'	The overture to 'Queen of Spades'
Эпило́г к дра́ме	Epilogue to a drama
Он сочиня́л му́зыку к фи́льмам	He composed music for films
Ключ к замку́ (cf. ключ к зага́дке 'the key to a riddle')	The key to a lock

(4) The dominant form denotes feeling, attitude, etc.:-

Ко мне относи́лись ина́че	They treated me differently
Она́ добра́ к ним	She is kind to them
Появля́лись пе́рвые про́блески интере́са к этимоло́гии	The first glimmerings of interest in etymology would appear
Жа́лость к себе́, не́нависть к Са́ше	Pity for herself, hatred for Sasha
Она́ равноду́шна к Кра́вченко	She is indifferent to Kravchenko
Он спосо́бен к му́зыке	He is good at music
Любо́вь к Отчи́зне	Love for the Fatherland

Other items include:-

Внима́тельный к, вражде́бный к, за́висть к, отвраще́ние к, отзы́вчивый к, отноше́ние к, почте́ние к, презре́ние к, пристра́стие к, ре́вность к, скло́нность к, сочу́вствие к, справедли́вый к, страсть к, стыть к	Considerate to, hostile to, envy for, aversion for, responsive to, attitude to, esteem for, contempt for, predilection for, jealousy of, inclination for, sympathy for, fair to, passion for, to cool towards

(5) The dominant form denotes preparation, readiness:-

Гото́в к труду́ и оборо́не	Ready for labour and defence
Гото́виться к отъе́зду	To prepare for departure

Preparation is also implied in:-

Стол, накры́тый к у́жину	A table laid for supper
Трениро́вались к спорти́вным состяза́ниям	They were training for a sports event

(6) The dominant form denotes suitability, designation, while the dependent noun is abstract or verbal:-

Го́дный к во́инской слу́жбе	Fit for military service
Маши́ны, предназна́ченные к ремо́нту	Cars ear-marked for repair
Приго́дный к употребле́нию	Fit for use

Other items include:-

Годи́ться к, приспоса́бливать(ся) к	To be fit for, to adapt (oneself) to

(7) The dependent noun denotes emotional reaction to an event, impression, etc.:-

К удово́льствию зри́телей, всё начало́сь снача́ла	To the spectators' pleasure, it began all over again
Сказа́ла, к его́ удивле́нию: – Не пое́ду	To his surprise, she said 'I shan't go'
К сча́стью, к сожале́нию	Fortunately, unfortunately

Other phrases include:-

К (вели́кой) доса́де, к (по́лному) негодова́нию, к (вели́кому) огорче́нию, к его́ у́жасу	To one's (great) annoyance, to one's (complete) indignation, to one's (absolute) mortification, to his horror, etc.

(8) In temporal contexts, the preposition means 'by':-

К ве́черу, к концу́ неде́ли	By evening, by the end of the week
К тому́ вре́мени, когда́ электри́чка подходи́ла к платфо́рме, шёл седьмо́й час его́ дежу́рства	By the time the electric train approached the platform, he had been on duty for over six hours

XV

OT + GENITIVE CASE

(1) The preposition's central meaning is 'away from' a place:-

Она́ отошла́ от окна́	She moved away from the window
Он шёл от реки́	He was walking from the river

or a person:-

Почему́ она́ ушла́ от му́жа?	Why did she leave her husband?
Письмо́ от до́чери	A letter from one's daughter

The dominant form may denote distance between two points:-

От го́рода до села́ 15 мину́т езды́	It is fifteen minutes' ride from the town to the village

(2) The dominant noun denotes (a) a detachable part of an object:-

Ключ от чемода́на	The key of the suitcase
Ле́звие от безопа́сной бри́твы	The blade from a safety razor

or (b) a receptacle:-

Футля́р от виолонче́ли; ба́ночка от ма́зи; цили́ндрик от губно́й пома́ды	A cello case; an ointment jar; a lipstick holder

(3) The dependent noun denotes source:-

(a) source of energy:-

Га́зовая пли́тка рабо́тает от балло́на со сжа́тым га́зом	The gas stove works off a cylinder of compressed gas
Увлажни́тель во́здуха пита́ется от дома́шней электросе́ти	The air moisturiser is powered by a domestic circuit

(b) origin, parentage:-

Сын от пе́рвого бра́ка	A son from the first marriage
Ребёнок, кото́рый роди́тся от же́нщины, на кото́рой вы	A child who will be born of the woman you promised to marry

обеща́ли жени́ться

(c) temporal source:-

Моё письмо́ от пе́рвого а́вгуста	My letter of August 1

(d) physical source, often with a nuance of cause:-

Воро́нка от бо́мбы	A bomb crater
Пожа́р от бро́шенной спи́чки	A fire caused by a discarded match

(4) Causal meanings. (a) The dependent noun denotes the physical cause of a state or process:-

Доро́га оказа́лась мо́крой от дождя́	The road turned out to be wet with rain
Боль от ожо́га	The pain from a burn
Он у́мер от ра́ка	He died of cancer

(b) the dominant item denotes an involuntary physical reaction to a feeling:-

Он вздыха́л от жа́лости	He was sighing with pity
Он запла́кал от ра́дости	He wept with joy
Дрожа́ть от стра́ха	To tremble with fear
Он покрасне́л от стыда́	He blushed with shame
Бле́дный от не́нависти	Pale with hatred

Other dependent nouns denoting feelings which may cause an involuntary reaction include:-

Любо́вь, наслажде́ние, негодова́ние, ро́бость, смуще́ние, расте́рянность	Love, enjoyment, indignation, shyness, embarrassment, confusion, etc., etc.

Cf. c + genitive case (13; page 72)

Note the causal phrase: от не́чего де́лать 'for want of something to do'

(5) The dominant form denotes protection:-

Защища́ть го́род от врага́	To defend the town against the enemy
Страхова́ть това́р от ри́ска	To insure goods against risk

The context may indicate 'riddance', 'evasion':-

Возде́рживаться от голосова́ния	To abstain from voting
Избавля́ться от привы́чки	To get rid of a habit
Она́ отказа́лась от мое́й по́мощи	She refused my help

Other items include:-

Отде́лываться от, отреша́ться от, свобо́дный от, спаса́ть от, удёрживаться от, уви́ливать от, уклоня́ться от	To dispose of, to renounce, free from, to save from to refrain from to evade, to avoid

The prepositional phrase also appears in 'curative' contexts:-

Лечи́ть ма́льчика от дифтери́та	To treat a boy for dyphtheria
Что у вас есть от бронхи́та?	What have you got for bronchitis?
Лека́рство от ка́шля	Cough medicine
Что помога́ет от пе́чени?	What is good for the liver?
Он вы́лечил больно́го от туберкулёза	He cured the patient of TB

Other items include:-

Крем от, мазь от, порошо́к от, противоя́дие от	Cream for, ointment for, powder for, an antidote for

(6) The dominant form denotes dependence:-

Это бу́дет зави́сеть от обстоя́тельств	That will depend on circumstances
Зави́симость ры́ночных цен от спро́са	The dependence of market prices on demand

XVI

ДЛЯ + GENITIVE CASE

(1) The preposition's central meaning is 'purpose'. The dependent noun may denote the purpose of an action, expressed:-

(a) by a verbal noun:-

Ехать в тыл для основа́тельного лече́ния	To travel to the rear for a thorough course of treatment

(b) by other nouns indicating action:-

По́дняли винто́вку для пе́рвого за́лпа	They raised their rifles for the first volley

(c) by a noun which indicates a deliberately-created impression:-

Он говори́л э́то для отво́да глаз	He was saying that to pull the wool over their eyes
Не́сколько мину́т он для ви́да поигра́л с ребя́тами	For a few minutes, for the sake of of appearances, he played with the children

Other prepositional phrases include:-

Для ви́димости, для профо́рмы, для эффе́кта	For appearance's sake, as a matter of form, for effect

(d) by a noun which indicates a state of mind:-

Всё гото́в сде́лать для её поко́я и сча́стья	He is prepared to do anything for her peace of mind and happiness
Это я для ве́рности спра́шиваю	I am asking just to make sure

(e) by a noun which indicates a physical state:-

Но́ги для удо́бства вы́тянул	He stretched out his legs for comfort

(f) by a noun which indicates distinction or variety:-

Его́ зва́ли по и́мени-о́тчеству, для отли́чки, так как жил ещё Фёдор Матёрин	They called him by his name and patronymic - to differentiate, since there was another Fedor Materin still living

Other prepositional phrases include для разнообра́зия 'for a change'

(g) by a noun which indicates a quality:-

Во второ́й или тре́тий раз для бо́льшей не́жности пропуска́л фарш через мясору́бку	He put the stuffing through the mincer for a second or third time for greater tenderness

(h) by a noun which indicates sensation or reaction:-

Нацепи́л на себя́ – для сме́ха – ю́бку ста́ршей сестры́	He pinned on his elder sister's skirt for a laugh

(i) by a noun which denotes abbreviation:-

Для кра́ткости звал их: Мои́ шесть же́нщин	He called them 'my six women' for short

(2) The dominant form denotes designation, suitability, relevance, etc. (the dependent noun may be verbal, abstract or may denote an object):-

Шкала́ си́мволов пого́ды предназна́чена для устано́вки вы́держки	The scale of weather symbols is designed for setting the exposure
Пи́ща, приго́дная для употребле́ния	Food, fit for consumption
Льди́на годи́тся для нау́чной ста́нции	The ice-floe is suitable for a scientific station
Ме́сто, го́дное для спу́ска самолёта	A place suitable for landing an aircraft
Су́дно, предназна́ченное для да́льних пла́ваний	A vessel destined for distant voyages

(3) The dependent noun is нача́ло:-

Для нача́ла пошёл посмотре́ть, как рабо́тает Ко́стя	For a start he went to see how Kostya was working

(4) The dominant form is a noun:-

Па́пка для бума́г	A file for papers
Пилю́ли для се́рдца	Heart tablets
Каби́нка для раздева́ния	A changing cubicle

(5) The dependent noun is animate:-

Общежи́тие для студе́нтов	A students' hostel
Она́ сняла́ ко́пию для Па́вла	She took a copy for Pavel

(6) The preposition appears in contexts with a comparative or relative meaning:-

Он опытен для своих лет	He is experienced for his years
Это был невероятно жаркий день для Прибалтики	For the Baltic coast it was an incredibly hot day

(7) The dependent noun denotes the object, state or person to which the dominant item relates:-

Непроницаемый для воды; вредный для здоровья	Waterproof; harmful for the health
Те семь дней весьма типичны для Запада	Those 7 days are extremely typical of the West

XVII

ДО + GENITIVE CASE

(1) The preposition's central meaning is 'up to', 'as far as':-

Этот автобус идёт только до станции	This bus goes only as far as the station

(2) In temporal contexts the meaning is 'before', 'until', etc.:-

До войны	Before the war
До того как он пришёл	Before he came
Ждать до вечера	To wait until evening
До тех пор; до недавнего времени; до сих пор	Until then; until recently; up to now
Ждите до тех пор, как он придёт	Wait until he comes
С часу до двух	From one o'clock to two

(3) The prepositional phrase may denote quantitative limit:-

Родители, имеющие до 5 человек детей	Parents having up to five children

(4) The preposition appears in many figurative combinations with the verbs доходить, доводить:-

Доходить до драки, до полного разложения	To end in a brawl, in complete disintegration
Доводить до отчаяния, до слёз	To reduce to despair, to tears

(5) The dependent noun denotes the result of an action, either in physical terms:-

Работать до изнеможения	To work to the point of exhaustion
Заставляли пациентов накуриваться до тошноты	They made the patients smoke to the point of nausea

or in mental terms:-

Маргóшка раздобы́ла лотó, и они́ игрáли до óдури	Margoshka got out the Bingo, and they played themselves into a stupor

(6) The dependent noun may denote an extreme form of the dominant item:-

До щепети́льности чéстная	Meticulously honest
Самоувéренный до нáглости	Self-confident to the point of arrogance

(7) The dependent noun denotes a change in state:-

Паркéт, натёртый до блéска	Parquet, polished to a high gloss
Загорéл почти до черноты́	He burnt almost black

(8) The dependent noun denotes the spatial limit of various processes and states:-

Онá покраснéла до ушéй	She blushed to the roots of her hair
Ногá ампути́рована до бедрá	The leg has been amputated to the hip
Онá былá в бéлом до пят плáтье	She was wearing a white ankle-length dress
Он улыбáлся до ушéй	He was smiling from ear to ear
Они́ раздéлись до белья́	They undressed to their underwear

Note the set phrases in the following examples:-

Промóк, промёрз до костéй	He got soaked, frozen right through
Он эгои́ст до мóзга костéй	He is an egoist to the core
Вооружённый до зубóв	Armed to the teeth

(9) The phrase до полови́ны denotes semi-completion:-

Две спи́чки до полови́ны сгорéли	The two matches half burnt out

(10) The dependent noun denotes minimal components (a) of a generalised nature:-

До детáлей продýманная рабóта	A piece of work which has been considered down to the last detail
Егó лицó, до мелочéй мне знакóмое	His face, familiar to me in intimate detail
Стёкла вы́биты все до одногó	Every one of the window panes has

been knocked out

and (b) of a more specific nature:-

Всё проверит до буковки	He will check everything down to the last letter
Выпили всё до (последней) капли	They drank everything down to the last drop
Он всю получку, до копейки, принёс домой	He brought all his pay home, down to the last kopeck
До (последней) нитки промокать	To get soaked to the skin

(11) The prepositional phrase can express precision:-

План, рассчитанный экономистами до секунд	A plan calculated by the economists down to the last second

(12) A number of phrases express general meanings of extent:-

До крайности, до предела, до некоторой степени, до такой степени	Extremely, boundlessly, to a certain extent, such an extent

Some phrases combine with specific types of dominant word:-

До зарезу нужно уточнить кое-какие детали	We badly need to define certain details more precisely
Наесться до отвалу	To eat one's fill
Зал набит до отказа	The hall is packed to capacity
Он до смерти устал	He is dead tired
Танцевать, смеяться до упаду	To dance, laugh to the point of exhaustion

XVIII

НАД + INSTRUMENTAL CASE

(1) The preposition's central meaning is 'above', 'over':-

Самолёт летит над городом	The aircraft is flying over the town

Note the figurative use in:-

Угроза, нависшая над страной	A threat hanging over the country

(2) The dominant form denotes 'dominance', 'control':-

Стоики умели властвовать над своими страстями	The Stoics knew how to control their passions
Победа над фашизмом	The victory over Fascism

Other items include:-

Брать верх над; контроль над; шефствовать над (детским садом)	To get the upper hand over; control of; to sponsor (a kindergarten)

as well as суд, эксперимент:-

Суд над Эйхманом	The trial of Eichmann
Он подозревал какой-то злой эксперимент над собой	He suspected some evil experiment on himself

(3) The dominant form denotes work, both practical and mental:-

Бились над усовершенствованием машин	They cudgelled their brains over the perfecting of the machines
Он работал над портретом, над романом	He was working on the portrait, on the novel

Other items include:-

Думать над, корпеть над, задумываться над, ломать голову над, размышлять над	To think about, to pore over, to ponder over, to rack one's brains over, to reflect on

(4) The dominant form denotes laughter, mockery, etc.:-

Она́ смеётся над мои́ми мечта́ми	She laughs at my dreams
Он издева́лся над мое́й руба́шкой	He mocked my shirt
Хихи́кают надо всем	They giggle at everything

Other items include:-

Злора́дствовать над, ирони- зи́ровать над	To gloat over, to speak ironic- ally of,
насмеха́ться над,	to jeer at,
подшу́чивать над,	to chaff,
потеша́ться над,	to make fun of,
труни́ть над	to mock (at)

(5) The dominant form is сжа́литься:-

Сжа́литься над несча́стным	To take pity on an unfortunate person

XIX

O + ACCUSATIVE CASE

(1) The dominant item denotes striking, collision, etc.:-

Му́ха бьётся о стекло́	The fly beats against the pane
Днепр разбива́ется о ка́мни поро́гов	The Dnieper smashes against the boulders of the rapids
Сбива́л пе́пел с папиро́сы о носо́к сапога́	He was knocking the ash from his cigarette against the toe of his boot
Спотыка́юсь о ка́мни	I trip over the stones
Уда́рился ного́й о стул	He struck his leg against the chair

Other items include:-

Выбива́ть тру́бку о, расплю́щивать о, сту́каться о	To knock out a pipe on, to flatten against, bang against

Note the idiom:-

Па́лец о па́лец не уда́рил	He did not do a stroke

(2) The dominant item denotes friction, pressure, etc.:-

Я вы́тер я́блоко о полу́ ку́ртки	I wiped the apple on the flap of my jacket
Он погаси́л сига́ру о подо́шву сапога́	He extinguished his cigar on the sole of his boot
Она́ гре́ла ладо́ни о ча́йник	She was warming her hands on the kettle
Обожжёшься об огонёк сигаре́ты	You will burn yourself on the cigarette
Ле́на оперла́сь о Па́влика спино́й	Lena leant up against Pavlik
Острека́лся о крапи́ву	He stung himself on some nettles

Запа́чкать ю́бку о ку́чи му́сора	To dirty one's skirt on piles of rubbish
Она́ уколо́лась о веретено́	She pricked herself on a spindle

Other items include:-

Обдира́ть о, облока́чиваться о, тере́ться о	To skin on, to lean on (against), to rub oneself against

Note the phrase бок о́ бок:-

Давно́ они́ уже́ не сиде́ли ря́дом, вот так, бок о́ бок	It was a long time since they had sat next to each other like this, side by side

(3) The dominant item denotes a sound caused by collision, friction, etc.:-

Ка́тер заскрипе́л дни́щем о ка́мни	The launch scraped its bottom on the stones
Ту́фли посту́кивают об асфа́льт	The shoes clatter on the asphalt
Камы́ш зашурша́л о борта́ челнока́	The reeds rustled against the sides of the boat
Скре́жет лопа́т о па́лубу	The scraping of the spades on the deck
Шум дождя́ о зе́млю	The noise of the rain against the earth

Other items include:-

Греме́ть о, позве́нькивать о, хлю́пать о	To rattle against, tinkle against, to squelch against

XX

O + PREPOSITIONAL CASE

(1) The dependent noun denotes the topic of thought and other mental processes:-

Ду́мать о пла́не	To think about the plan
Напомина́ть о до́лге	To remind someone of his duty
Поня́тие о меща́нстве	The concept of philistinism
'О происхожде́нии ви́дов'	'On the Origin of Species'

Other items include:-

Воспомина́ние о, мечта́ о, мысль о, по́мнить о, упомина́ть о	Recollection of, a dream of, a thought of, to remember about, to mention

Note also usage with вопро́с, де́ло, зако́н:-

Вопро́с о европе́йском совеща́нии	The question of a European conference
Слу́шается де́ло об убийстве	A murder case is being heard
Зако́н о разво́де, о клевете́	Divorce law, law on slander

and with words denoting command, proposal:-

Предложе́ние об убо́рке урожа́я	A proposal for gathering in the harvest
Прика́з об отступле́нии	The order for retreat

Other items include догова́риваться о 'to agree about', постановле́ние о 'a decree for'

(2) The dominant form denotes request:-

Про́сьба о деньга́х	A request for money
Призы́в о по́мощи	An appeal for help
Заявле́ние ГДР о прие́ме её в ООН	The GDR's application for admission to the UNO
Проси́ли о снисхожде́нии	They asked for indulgence

Other items include молѝтва о 'a prayer for (something)', молѝть-
ся о 'to pray for (something)', умоля́ть о 'to beg for'

(3) The dominant form denotes care, concern:-

Забо́та о дере́вьях	Care for the trees
Забо́титься·о ве́чере самоде́ятель-ности	To see about an amateur concert

Other items include хлопота́ть о 'to see about', ходáтайствовать
о 'to petition for'.

(4) An attributive meaning is retained in certain set expressions:-

Пáлка о двух концáх; конь о четырёх ногáх, да споты́ка́ется	A two-edged weapon; anyone can make a mistake

XXI

ПЕРЕД + INSTRUMENTAL CASE

(1) The preposition's central meaning is 'in front of':-

Он стоял перед домом	He was standing in front of the house

Note figurative usage in the following:-

Перед нами большая задача	A major task confronts us
Представать перед судом	To come to trial

(2) The temporal meaning is 'just before':-

Перед отъездом, перед едой, перед сном	Just before departure, before meals, before going to bed
Как всегда перед Олимпиадой, не было недостатка в прогнозах	As always before the Olympics, there was no lack of forecasts

(3) The prepositional phrase combines with a number of dominant forms which denote (i) guilt:-

Я виноват перед вами	I owe you an apology

Other items include:-

Провиниться перед	To do wrong to

(ii) exculpation:-

Он извинился передо мной	He apologised to me

Other items include:-

Оправдываться перед,	To justify oneself in someone's eyes,
реабилитировать перед	to rehabilitate in someone's eyes

(iii) responsibility, duty:-

Я в великом долгу перед ним	I owe him a great debt

Мы в отве́те не то́лько перед на́шей со́вестью, но и перед все́ми людьми́	We are responsible not only to our consciences, but to all people

Other items include:-

Отве́тственность перед, отвеча́ть перед, отчи́тываться перед	Responsibility to, to be respon- sible to, to report back to

(iv) fear, awe:-

Сму́тный страх перед ма́терью	A vague fear of mother
Благогове́ть перед па́мятью кого́-то	To revere someone's memory

Other items include:-

Преклоня́ться перед, робе́ть перед, трясти́сь перед	To worship, to quail before, to tremble before

(v) faint-heartedness, surrender:-

Отступа́ть перед опа́сностью	To retreat in the face of danger
Зага́дки, перед кото́рыми нау́ка пасу́ет	Enigmas shirked by science

(vi) humility, helplessness:-

Мы беспо́мощны перед сме́ртью	We are helpless in the face of death

Other items include беccи́льный перед 'powerless in the face of'

(vii) embarrassment, confusion:-

Ему́ бы́ло сты́дно перед сами́м собо́й	He was ashamed of himself
Растеря́нность перед её красото́й и великоду́шием	Confusion in the face of her beauty and magnanimity

Other items include:-

Нело́вко, неудо́бно перед, смуще́ние перед, срами́ть перед, стесня́ться перед	Ill at ease, awkward in front of, embarrassment before, to disgrace in front of, to be shy in front of

(viii) pretence:-

Притворя́юсь перед сами́м собо́й	I am pretending to myself

Other items include де́лать вид перед 'to pretend to, in front of', хитри́ть перед 'to put on an act in front of'

(ix) ingratiation:-

Уго́дничать перед си́льным	To cringe before the strong
Низкопокло́нство перед За́падом	Servility towards the West

Other items include:-

Выслуживаться перед,	To curry favour with,
заискивать перед,	to ingratiate oneself with,
пресмыкаться перед	to crawl to

(x) pride, arrogance:-

Высокомерная перед публикой	Arrogant towards the public

Other items include красоваться перед 'to show off in front of'

(xi) defiance, resolution:-

Ни перед чем не останавливаются	They stop at nothing
Стойкость перед соблазном	Steadfastness in the face of temptation

Other items include:-

Непокорённость, спокойствие перед, устоять перед	Indomitability, composure in the face of, to resist

(xii) advocacy:-

Редакция ходатайствовала перед Союзом писателей о направлении его в эту командировку	The editorial board appealed to the Union of Writers to send him on this business trip

(xiii) preference:-

Отдал Киеву предпочтение перед Одессой	He gave Kiev preference over Odessa
У человека перед компьютером нет преимуществ	A man has no advantages over a computer

(xiv) miscellaneous meanings:-

Все равны перед опасностью •	All are equal in the face of danger
Быть честным перед собой	To be honest to oneself
Люди, чистые перед партией и перед народом	People unsullied in the eyes of the party and the people
Перед этим подвигом бледнеют все остальные	All other exploits pale by comparison with this one

XXII

ПО + ACCUSATIVE CASE

(1) The preposition's central meaning is 'up to and including'
(a) a point in space. The dependent noun is often part of the
body:-

Обнажённая по локоть рука́	An arm bared to the elbow
По щи́колотку стоя́ла вода́	The water was up to their ankles

Other parts of the body commonly found as dependent nouns in the
construction include:-

Бедро́, го́рло, грудь, коле́но, пле́чи, у́ши	Hip, throat, chest, knee, shoulders, ears

Note idiomatic usage in the following:-

За́нят по го́рло; сыт по го́рло	Up to one's eyes in work; fed up to the teeth
Влюбля́ться по́ уши; по́ уши в долга́х; красне́ть по́ уши	To fall madly in love; up to the ears in debt; to blush to the roots of one's hair
Мо́ре ему́ по коле́но	He doesn't give a damn

and usage with other items:-

Дома́, по о́кна погружённые в снег	Houses buried up to the windows in snow

(b) a point in time:-

Бу́ду там по деся́тое	I shall be there up to and including the tenth
С ию́ня по сентя́брь	From June to September inclusive

Compare до + genitive case (2), (8), pages 100, 101

(2) The preposition combines in meaning of location with the
nouns рука́ and сторона́:-

Он сиди́т по одну́ сто́рону перегоро́дки, а она́ стои́т по другу́ю сто́рону	He sits on one side of the partition, and she stands on the other

По ле́вую и по пра́вую ру́ку от   The sons were sitting to the left
отца́ сиде́ли сыновья́   and right of their father

Other phrases include:-

По ту сто́рону, по э́ту сто́рону,   On that side, this side,
по ле́вую сто́рону, по пра́вую   the left side, the right side,
сто́рону, по о́бе сторо́ны   on both sides
(also: по обе́им сторона́м)

(3) In distributive meanings, по + accusative case is used with
the numerals 2-4 (for usage with the numeral 1, see по + dative
case 8, pages 117-118):-

Мы вы́пили по́ две ча́шки   We drank two cups each

and with the numerals 200, 300 and 400 (500-900 appear either in
a special form: по пятисо́т ... or in an accusative or unmarked
form: по пятьсо́т ...)

In written Russian, many Soviet grammarians advocate the use of
по + the dative case of the numerals 5-100 for the expression of
distributive meanings, assigning по + accusative case to the
colloquial register. However, Skvortsov (1980): 176-177 writes
in reference to distributive constructions of this type:-

> It must be said that the accusative case with <u>po</u> is
> extending more and more from spoken to written Russian
> and is gradually supplanting constructions with the
> dative.

Itskovich (1977): 227 also refers to the spread of collocations
of the type по пять in place of the type по пяти́, for the expression of distributive meaning.

Examples from contemporary literature show that both types of
distributive phrase are used: (a) по + dative case:-

Приходи́лось рабо́тать по   We had to work 12 hours a day
двена́дцати часо́в в день

По десяти́ ты́сяч в ба́нке стоя́ло   They had ten thousand each in the
                                  bank

and (b) по + accusative case:-

За стола́ми нас сиде́ло по   At each of the tables sat 10-16
де́сять-шестна́дцать курса́нтов of us students

Все рабо́тают по семь часо́в в   Everybody works seven hours a day
су́тки

40, 90 and 100 are found mainly in the accusative case (or what
some grammarians term an 'affixless' or undeclined form):-

Они́ стоя́ли шере́нгами, по́ сто в   They were standing in rows, a
шере́нге   hundred in each row

Indefinite numerals are found both in the dative:-

| Слова́ име́ют по не́скольку значе́ний | The words have several meanings each |

and in the accusative:-

| Он сказа́л сестре́, чем его́ пои́ть и по ско́лько | He told the nurse what to give him to drink and how much at a time |

(4) The dependent noun denotes the object of fetching (cf. за + instrumental case 4, pages 74-75), mainly in the colloquial or demotic registers. The range of nouns include вода́ 'water', грибы́ 'mushrooms', дрова́ 'firewood', мали́на 'raspberries', and some others:-

| Весно́й хо́дят де́вушки в ро́щу по ла́ндыши, ле́том - по я́годы | In spring the girls go to the copse for lily-of-the-valley, in the summer - for berries |

XXIII

ПО + DATIVE CASE

(1) The preposition's central meaning is 'over the surface of', 'along', etc.:-

По бе́регу, по во́здуху, по Во́лге, по направле́нию к,	Along the bank, through the air, down the Volga, in the direction of,
по́ полу, по пути́ (доро́ге), вверх по тече́нию, вниз по тече́нию	over the floor, on the way, upstream, downstream
Спуска́ться по ле́стнице	To go downstairs
Он провёл руко́й по волоса́м	He ran his hand through his hair
Ка́пли дождя́ стека́ют по стеклу́	Rain drops stream down the pane
Он шёл по мосту́ через Неву́	He was crossing the bridge over the Neva
'Сою́з-29' дви́жется по орби́те	'Soyuz-29' moves along its orbit
По пути́ домо́й	On the way home

Movement may be multi-directional:-

Они́ ката́лись по кру́гу	They were skating in a circle
Меня́ вози́ли по Болга́рии	I was driven round Bulgaria
Они́ бе́гают по ко́мнате	They are running round the room

When the noun is qualified by весь, the meaning is 'all over':-

По всей стране́ начала́сь убо́рка урожа́я	Harvesting has begun all over the country
- Я тебя́ по всей шко́ле ищу́	'I have been looking for you all over the school'

(2) The dependent noun denotes various points in space:-

Пе́репись населе́ния провели́ по всем населённым пу́нктам	The census was carried out in all built-up areas
По стена́м висе́ли порте́ты	Portraits of first-rate workers

передовико́в   hung round the walls

(3) The dependent noun denotes a number of destinations or goals :-

Весь день я ходи́л по магази́нам   I walked round the shops all day

Он разли́л конья́к по рю́мкам   He poured brandy into the glasses

Давно́ все разошли́сь по дома́м   Everyone has long ago dispersed
                                     to their homes

(4) The dependent noun denotes a line or means of communication:-

По желе́зной доро́ге, по по́чте,   By rail, by mail,
по ра́дио, по телеви́зору,   on the radio, on television,
по телефо́ну   on the telephone

По ра́дио передава́ли, что   They announced on the radio that
но́чью бу́дет 35 гра́дусов   there would be 35 degrees of frost
моро́за   that night

Он смотре́л по второ́й програ́мме   He was watching an ice-hockey
хокке́йный матч   match on channel two

(5) The prepositional phrase conveys meanings of accordance. English equivalents vary widely:-

По пра́ву, по происхожде́нию,   By right, by origin,
по прика́зу, по тео́рии вероя́т-   by order, by the law of averages
ностей

Реше́ния принима́ются по   Decisions are taken by a majority
большинству́ голосо́в   of votes

По мои́м часа́м оди́ннадцать   By my watch it is eleven

По пла́ну,   According to the plan,
по расписа́нию,   according to the timetable,
по слу́ху   according to rumour

По стари́нному ру́сскому обы́чаю   We sit down, in accordance with
сади́мся   an old Russian custom

По до́лгу слу́жбы, по мне́нию,   In the course of duty, in the
                                     opinion of,
по-мо́ему, по о́череди,   in my opinion, in turn,
по сравне́нию с   in comparison with

По приглаше́нию, по про́сьбе   At the invitation of, at the re-
                                     quest of

По настоя́нию отца́ я занима́юсь   At my father's insistence I go in
физкульту́рой   for physical training

По па́мяти   From memory

А уро́ки? - опя́ть по привы́чке   'What about the homework?', Ira
спроси́ла Ира   asked again, from force of habit

По вкýсу   To taste

Note also the following usage:-

40 грáдусов по Цéльсию; фильм по ромáну; платѝть по счёту; покупáть по (льгóтным) цéнам;	40 degrees Centigrade; the film of the novel; to pay a bill; to buy at (preferential) prices;
по часовóй стрéлке (cf. прóтив часовóй стрéлки 'anticlockwise');	clockwise;
дéлать по-свóему	to get one's own way

(6) The dominant form denotes 'familiarity', 'judgement', etc.:-

Он знал всех телефонѝсток по голосáм	He knew all the operators by their voices
Я пóнял по егó лицý, какóе впечатлéние произвелá на негó пóлька	I saw from his face what an impression the Polish girl had made on him
Судѝть о кóм-нибудь по внéшности	To judge someone by their appearance

(7) The prepositional phrase denotes recurrent points in time:-

По утрáм, по вечерáм, по ночáм	In the mornings, in the evenings, at night time
По понедéльникам, по прáздникам,	On Mondays, on holidays,
по бýдням, по выходны́м дням (cf. в + accusative case, 14(b), pages 33-34)	on weekdays, on days off
Стоя́нка разрешáется по чётным (нечётным) дням	Parking is allowed on even (odd) days

The dependent noun may be qualified by цéлый to denote temporal continuity:-

По цéлым дням, по цéлым недéлям, по цéлым часáм	For days on end, weeks on end, for hours on end

(8) In distributive meanings the preposition combines with the dative of singular nouns and the numeral 1:-

В 25.8% семéй по одномý ребёнку	25.8% of families have one child
Учѝтель дал кáждому по кнѝге	The teacher gave each of them a book

For the use of the preposition with other numerals, see по + accusative case (3, pages 113-114)

The construction may also be used in singulative meaning:-

Падал редкий, по одной снежинке, снег	There was a light snowfall, with the odd flake here and there
Она пересмотрела все письма, по одному	She looked through all the letters, one by one

(9) The dependent noun denotes the object of actions of striking, throwing, shooting:-

По трём мишеням из трёх винтовок стреляют	They fire three rifles at the three targets
Он хлопнул меня по плечу	He clapped me on the shoulder
Открыли огонь по линкору	They opened fire on the battle-ship
Удары по мячу	Kicks at the ball

Other dominant forms include бить 'to strike', бросать 'to throw'

(10) The dependent noun denotes the object of yearning, grieving, etc.:-

Я так соскучился по солнцу	I so missed the sun
Тоска по родине	Homesickness
Она лила горькие слёзы по корове	She wept bitter tears over the cow

Other items include:-

Горевать по, панихида по, плакать по, томиться по, тосковать по, траур по	To grieve for, a requiem for, to weep for, to yearn for, to pine for, mourning for

(11) The dependent noun denotes 'business':-

Еду в город по делу (делам)	I am going to town on business

(12) The prepositional phrase denotes cause. The dependent noun indicates (a) cause, motive:-

По финансовым соображениям	For financial considerations
По какой причине вы это сделали?	For what reason did you do that?
По какому поводу вы об этом вспомнили?	What made you think of that?

(b) physical handicap:-

Галя по близорукости не заметила моего исчезновения	Due to her short-sightedness Galya did not notice my disappearance
По слабости здоровья он почти не покидает города	Because of poor health he scarcely leaves the town

Other phrases include по боле́зни 'due to sickness', по дря́хлости 'due to decrepitude'

(c) age (with implications of immaturity, infirmity, etc.):-

Нигде́ уже́ не рабо́тал по ста́рости	He had stopped working due to old age
Сын по мо́лодости не понима́ет его́	His son does not understand him due to his youth

Other phrases include по малоле́тству 'due to extreme youth'

(d) mental characteristics:-

Ма́льчик э́то сде́лал по глу́пости, по небре́жности, по невнима́тельности	The boy did this out of stupidity, carelessness, inattentiveness
По засте́нчивости свое́й он выбира́л са́мые тёмные углы́	In his shyness he would choose the darkest corners

Other phrases include:-

По забы́вчивости;	Due to forgetfulness;
по легкомы́слию; по ле́ности;	due to thoughtlessness; to laziness;
(жени́ться) по любви́; по найвности;	(marry) for love; due to naivete;
по нео́пытности; по неуме́нию;	due to inexperience; to inability;
по рассе́янности; по ску́пости;	due to absentmindedness; to meanness;
по ту́пости; по хала́тности	due to obtuseness; to negligence

(e) mistake, fault, ignorance:-

По вине́ води́теля происхо́дит 8 ава́рий из 10	8 out of 10 road accidents are due to driver error
Эти кни́ги по недосмо́тру заваля́лись под шка́фом	Due to an oversight these books lay around under the cupboard
По оши́бке	By mistake

Other phrases include:-

По неве́жеству, по незнако́мству,	Due to ignorance, to unfamiliarity,
по недоразуме́нию,	due to a misunderstanding,
по неосведомлённости	due to unawareness

(f) need:-

Он лишь по необходи́мости забега́л в теа́тр	It was only out of necessity that he would drop into the theatre

Other phrases include по на́добности 'out of need', по нужде́ 'out of necessity'

(g) various types of involuntary cause:-

Мы продолжа́ли по ине́рции	We continued mechanically to

разраба́тывать разли́чные прое́кты	devise various schemes
Де́йствовать по интуи́ции	To act on intuition
У него́ по счастли́вой случа́йности там име́лся прия́тель	By a lucky chance he had a friend there

Other phrases include:-

| По безвы́ходности, по волше́бству, по иро́нии судьбы́ | For lack of an alternative, by magic, by an irony of fate |

(13) The dependent noun defines the sphere of reference or activity of (a) persons:-

Специали́ст по перерабо́тке пластма́сс	A specialist in the processing of plastics
Чемпио́н по бо́ксу	A boxing champion
Инжене́р по профе́ссии	An engineer by profession
Това́рищ по ору́жию	A comrade in arms
По национа́льности армяни́н	By nationality an Armenian

(b) groups:-

| Комите́т по разоруже́нию | Disarmament committee |
| Отря́д по борьбе́ с алкоголи́змом | Anti-alcohol squad |

(c) organisations:-

| Заво́д по сбо́рке автомоби́лей | A car-assembly plant |

(d) activities:-

| Мероприя́тия по зашите от загрязне́ния во́здуха | Anti-air-pollution measures |

(e) mental activities and their products:-

План по вы́пуску	Production plan
Она́ сдава́ла экза́мен по исто́рии	She took a history exam
Ле́кции по фи́зике	Physics lectures

(f) printed materials:-

| Докуме́нты по мобилиза́ции | Mobilisation papers |
| Зада́чник по а́лгебре | A book of algebra problems |

(g) mechanisms:-

| Аппара́т по произво́дству азо́тной кислоты́ | An apparatus for the production of nitric acid |

(h) qualities, characteristics:-

| Сло́во кво́рум - лати́нское по | The work 'quorum' is Latin in |

происхождению	origin
Лекции интересны по форме и содержанию	The lectures are interesting in form and content

(i) ordinal numerals denoting order of preference or size:-

Африка второй по величине материк	Africa is the second largest continent
Антенна станет третьей по высоте в Европе	The antenna will be the third highest in Europe
Четвёртое в мире по глубине озеро	The fourth deepest lake in the world

XXIV

ПРИ + LOCATIVE/PREPOSITIONAL CASE

(1) The preposition's central meaning could be defined as 'in the presence of', 'close to'. It is used in some contexts of proximity:-

Да́ча стоя́ла при доро́ге	The villa stood near the road
Ло́дочную ста́нцию постро́или при слия́нии двух рек	The boating station was built at the confluence of two rivers

and can combine with the names of the sites of battles:-

Би́тва при Ка́ннах, при Бородине́, при Сталингра́де, бой при Цуси́ме	The battle of Cannae, Borodino, Stalingrad, Tsushima

(2) The preposition denotes 'attached to', in reference to (a) places:-

При университе́те есть поликли́ника	There is a clinic attached to the university

(b) persons:-

Адъюта́нт при главнокома́ндующем	An adjutant attached to the commander-in-chief

(3) The prepositional phrase can indicate availability:-

Сам я могу́ угости́ть, когда́ при деньга́х	I can stand drinks myself when I am flush

The dependent noun may be animate:-

Парашю́т, кото́рый всегда́ при лётчике	The parachute which a pilot always carries with him
У него́ при себе́ все бума́ги	He has all the documents on him

(4) The preposition means 'in the presence of':-

При студе́нтах он всегда́ называ́ет меня́ по и́мени-о́тчеству	In front of students he always calls me by my name and patronymic

(5) The preposition can denote 'in the lifetime of', 'in the reign of':-

Галилею при жизни не поставили памятника	No monument was erected to Galileo during his lifetime
При княгине Ольге Киевская Русь считалась королевством	During the reign of Princess Olga Kievan Rus was considered to be a kingdom

(6) The dependent noun denotes a social, political or economic system:-

Каким будет молодой человек при коммунизме?	What will a young person be like under Communism?
При советской власти, при империализме, при капитализме, при нэпе, при плановом хозяйстве, при социализме	Under Soviet power, under imperialism, under capitalism, under NEP, under a planned economy, under socialism

(7) The dependent noun denotes a source of light:-

При свете фонарика я распечатал конверт	I unsealed the envelope by the light of a torch
При свечах	By candle light
Нельзя смотреть скульптуру при электричестве (при электрическом освещении)	You should not examine sculpture by electric light
При свете дня, при дневном освещении	By day light

(8) The preposition combines with a verbal or abstract noun in temporal meaning:-

При взлёте уровень шумов его двигателей достигал 112 децибел	On take-off the engine noise reached 112 decibels
Плакал при малейшем напоминании о России	He would weep at the slightest mention of Russia
Задержанные при попытке удрать из-под надзора родителей	Apprehended in the attempt to escape from their parents' supervision

The preposition also combines with the nouns вид, звук, мысль, слово:-

При виде Петрова мальчик оживился	At the sight of Petrov the boy perked up
При первых звуках его голоса смолкают разговоры	At the first sounds of his voice conversations cease

| При одно́й мы́сли появи́ться перед ним лицо́ её залива́ла кра́ска | At the mere thought of appearing before him the blood rushed to her face |

(9) The preposition combines with the nouns возмо́жность, слу́чай:-

| При пе́рвой возмо́жности, при ка́ждой возмо́жности | At the first opportunity, at every opportunity |
| Я реши́л при слу́чае расспроси́ть его́ о кни́ге | I decided to question him about the book as soon as I got the chance |

(10) The preposition combines with abstract nouns in the meaning 'in view of', 'because of':-

| При её обая́нии не ка́ждая же́нщина помеша́ла бы ей блиста́ть | With her charm not every woman would be able to prevent her from standing out |
| При его́ зва́нии и положе́нии на́до быть демократи́чным | In view of his title and position he has to be democratic |

(11) Where the dependent noun is qualified by весь, the meaning of the prepositional phrase may be 'despite':-

| При всей свое́й наблюда́тельности он не заме́тил черни́льного пятна́ | For all his powers of observation he did not notice the ink stain |
| При всей свое́й вне́шней торопли́вости она́ никогда́ не спеши́ла | For all her outward haste she never hurried |

Note also при всём жела́нии 'with the best will in the world'

(12) The dependent noun denotes circumstances, in general terms:-

| При каки́х обстоя́тельствах он попа́л в плен? | In what circumstances was he taken prisoner? |
| При про́чих ра́вных усло́виях | All other things being equal |

or in more specific terms:-

Переходи́ть у́лицу при кра́сном све́те	To cross the street on a red light
При закры́той две́ри, при закры́тых дверя́х	Behind closed doors
При температу́ре 60°; при то́чке кипе́ния, то́чке замерза́ния	At a temperature of 60°; at boiling point, freezing point

Note the set phrase при жела́нии 'at will'

(13) The dependent noun denotes 'aid', etc.:-

| При по́мощи, при соде́йствии, | With the aid of, with the co-operation of, |

при уча́стии	with the participation of
Соглаше́ние гото́вится при посре́дстве 'Совиспа́на'	The agreement is being drawn up through the mediation of 'Sovispan'

(14) Phrases which denote the relevance or irrelevance of items in a statement:-

При чём здесь Англия? Он ру́сский	What has England to do with it? He is Russian
Твёрдость хара́ктера ни при чём	Firmness of character is irrelvant

(15) The phrase при э́том refers to supplementary or concomitant circumstances:-

Диа́метр ку́пола достига́л 43 м., при э́том толщина́ его́ доходи́ла до 2 м.	The diameter of the dome was 43 m., its thickness attaining 2 m.

XXV

C + INSTRUMENTAL CASE

(1) The preposition's central meaning is 'together with':-

Свяжи́те меня́ с дире́ктором	Put me in touch with the director
Косми́ческий кора́бль состыко-ва́лся с косми́ческой ста́нцией	The space ship rendezvoused with the space station

Some dominant verbs denote reciprocal or joint action:-

Дели́ться с, здоро́ваться с, проща́ться с, соглаша́ться с, ссо́риться с	To share with, to greet, to say goodbye to, to agree with, to quarrel with, etc.

The use of the preposition may be purely formal, for example, in combination with the verb расстава́ться 'to part with'. Cf. also:-

Хочу́ развести́сь с му́жем	I want to divorce my husband

Nouns and pronouns may combine as follows:-

Мы с ва́ми; они́ с сестро́й; оте́ц с ма́терью	You and I; he and his sister; father and mother

In combination with the name of an object, the meaning is often 'holding', etc.:-

Са́ша лежа́л с карандашо́м в зуба́х	Sasha was lying with a pencil between his teeth

or 'characterised by':-

Челове́к с краси́вым лицо́м	A man with a handsome face

The dependent noun may denote content:-

Мешо́к с мукой, буты́лка с водо́й	A sack of flour, a bottle of water

The preposition may link paired objects:-

Хлеб с ма́слом, омле́т с ветчино́й	Bread and butter, ham omelette

An abstract dependent noun may denote (i) concomitant circumstances, characteristics:-

Читáть с интерéсом, с удовóльствием, говорúть с акцéнтом, находúть с трудóм ...	To read with interest, with pleasure to speak with an accent, to find with difficulty, etc.

Cf. also:-

Дверь с шýмом отворúлась	The door opened with a crash

(ii) a meaning of purpose:-

Обращáться с прóсьбой	To make a request
Дéлать с намéрением	To do with a purpose
В Прáгу вúехала с дрýжеским визúтом делегáция совéтских профсоúзов	A Soviet trade union delegation has left on a friendly visit to Prague

(iii) the meaning of content:-

Письмó с жáлобой	A letter of complaint
Заявлéние с прóсьбой о принýтии в комсомóл	An application for admission to the Komsomol

(2) The preposition combines with the noun пóмощь (cf. also при + locative case 13, pages 124-125):-

Разговóр вёлся с пóмощью переводчика	The conversation was conducted with the help of an interpreter
С пóмощью инструмéнтов	With the aid of instruments

(3) The preposition combines with the noun скóрость:-

Он éхал со скóростью в пять киломéтров в минýту	He was travelling at a speed of five kilometres a minute

(4) The prepositional phrase functions as the grammatical object of a number of verbs:-

Борóться с зáсухой	To struggle against the drought
Поздравлýть с успéхом (cf. с Нóвым гóдом! Happy New Year!)	To congratulate on success
Справлýться с задáчей	To cope with a task
Обращáться с ружьём	To handle a gun

It also combines with a number of items which denote 'occurrence', 'state', etc.:-

Что случúлось с ним?	What has happened to him?
У менý с сéрдцем плóхо	I have heart trouble
Им с деньгáми трýдно	They have money problems
Катастрóфа с самолётом	A plane disaster

Other dominant items include:-

Авария, инцидент, случай, затяжка, неполадки	Accident, incident, occurrence, delay, trouble

(5) The dependent noun denotes the object of certain feelings and attitudes:-

Хорошо обращаться с кем-нибудь	To treat someone kindly
Я была с вами груба	I was rude to you
Лара любезна со всеми	Lara is nice to everyone
Подзащитные, с которыми суд был строг	Defendants the court was hard on
Он становился с Ларисой всё холоднее и холоднее	He was becoming colder and colder to Larissa

Other dominant items include:-

Вежливый с, ласковый с, надменный с, откровенный с, приветливый с, сдержанный с	Polite to, affectionate towards, haughty with, frank with, affable with, reserved towards

(6) In temporal meaning, the preposition appears (a) in phrases meaning 'in due course, eventually':-

Это у него с годами (со временем) пройдёт	He will grow out of it in time

(b) in combination with items denoting 'interval':-

Стал с небольшими перерывами звонить раз за разом	He began to ring again and again, at short intervals

INDEX OF ENGLISH PREPOSITIONS

Arabic numerals denote pages in the monograph. Capitalised non-underlined words denote categories of meaning (CAUSE, PLACE, etc.). Two dots (..) denote 'etc.'

BECAUSE OF 82, 118.

BEFORE
    TIME 100, 109, (also 80-81)
    Before the eyes 13; before leaving 32; before retiring 60.
    Appear before the court 21; embarrassment, tremble before ..
    110.

BEHIND
    PLACE 73, 77.
    Behind closed doors 124.

BETWEEN 24.

BEYOND 73.

BY
    PLACE 89.
    TIME 93.
    SEIZING, GRASPING (take by ..) 78.
    By chance 120; by comparison 111; by ear 63-64; by irony
120; by the law of averages 116; by the light 123; by magic 120;
by mail 116; by a majority 116; by means of 130; by mistake 119;
by nationality 120; by order 116; by origin 116; by profession
120; by rail 116; by right 116; by a watch 116.
    Begin by 71; increase by 63; judge by 117; know by 117; learn
by 49; multiply by 61; powered by 94; support by 78, 86; under-
stand by 83.
    Assailed by doubts 31; one by one .. 118; side by side 106.

DOWN
    Down the mine 21; down the Volga .. 115.

DURING 24, 35, 80.
    During a lifetime, reign 123.

FOR
    TIME 36, 62, 71, 81, 117.
    CAUSE 43, 72, 75, 95, 118, 119, 120.
    FEELING (pity for ..) 92.
    PROXY (decide for ..) 78-79.
    PURPOSE 97-98.
    RELATIVE (hot for the Baltic) 99.
    For all (her haste ..) 124; for appearances 97; for a bet 66;
for a change 98; for confirmation .. 60; for effect 97; for firewood .. 61; for a joke 40; for the journey, road .. 32, 60; for
lack of 75, 120; for a laugh 98; for love 119; for a meal 58; for
a motive 43; for a present 62; for a reason 72, 118; for repair ..
32; for scrap .. 32; for short 98; for spare parts 61; for a start
98; for want of something to do 95.
    Accept for 33; afraid for 79; allocate for 58, 86; ambition
for 91; apparatus for 120; appeal for 75, 107; application for
107; apply for 29; appropriate for 86; arrange for 62; arrangements for 32; ask for 107; beg for 108; blame for 26; buy for 64;
call for 74; care for 108; check for 59; cheque for 63; compete

for 79; competition for 58; a contract for 60; decree for 107;
demand for 62; designed .. for 58, 98; die for 79; dissertation
for 58; earmarked for 93; enlist for 55; exchange for 66; extend
for 56; fashion for 62; fear for 79; fight for 79; fit for 93, 98;
getting on for 87; glad for 79; go .. for 74-75, 114; go-ahead for
60; go bail for 60; good for 53, 60-61, 96; grieve .. for 118;
harmful for 99; hope for 65; insurance for 63; intercede for 79;
keep for 75; laid for 92; leave for 29, 56; look around for 75;
love for 92; material for 58; medicine .. for 96; money for 58;
need .. for 27, 66; an order for 62, 107; pay for 79; petition for
79, 108; play for 66; pray for 79, 108; prepare for 92; prepared
for 57; prescription for 60; proposal for 107; prospecting for 59;
punish for 80; queue for 66, 74; ready for 92; request for 107;
requisition for 60; reserve for 75; responsible for 79; save up
for 58; schedule of aircraft for 55; sell for 79; set out for 57;
sign for 26; signal for 91; submit for 60; suitable for 98; take
for 80; test for 58-59; thank .. for 80; ticket for 55; train for
92; treat for 96; try for 80; vote for 79; vouch for 79; warrant
for 60; work for 59; worried for 79; yearn for 118.

FROM

PLACES 42, 67-69, 82, 94.

From abroad 82; from the air 68; from all over 69; from an
armchair 68; from bed 68; from behind 82; from the ceiling 83;
from the end 42, 68; from the eyes 42, 69; from the field 68;
from a flat 42; from a height 68; from the kitchen 42; from the
navy 69; from near 88; from outside .. 82; from the sea 69; from
the sky 68; from the table 82; from under 88; from a vehicle 42,
68; from the yard 68.

From place to place 42, 69.

TIME 70, 71, 100	CAUSE (pain .. from) 72, 95.
EVENTS (from the war ..) 69-70	DISTANCE 94
SOURCE 94-95	PERSON 70, 94
STATE 42, 88.	

From custody, influence .. 88; from ear to ear 101; from
force of habit 116; from life 70; from memory 116.

Abstain from 95; borrow from 89; buy .. from 89, 90; a copy
from 70; free from 96; learn from 90; prepare from 49; refrain
from 96; save from 96; see from 117; shoot from 43; steal from 90;
translation from 70; win from 90.

IN

PLACES, BUILDINGS, ORGANISATIONS 9-11, 44-48, 63, 115.

In the air 12; in an apartment 13, 14; in one's arm(s) 19,
30; in an armchair 21; in the attic 44; in the balcony 45; in bed
14-15; in a, the circle 45, 115; in clothes 12; in one's country
46, 89; in the country 73; in country areas 20; in the department
18, 44; in the depths 13; in a direction 21, 55-56, 115; in s.o.'s
ear 30; in the eyes (also fig.) 12, 109, 111; in the faculty 44,
45; in a, the field(s) 18; in a foreign clime 46; in a frying-pan
47; in the gallery 45; in one's hand(s) 19, 30; in the heights 12;
in the kitchen 15; in the light (also fig.) 19; in the margin 18;

in the market garden 18; in the middle 19; in the navy 20; in the
NSEW 45; in orbit 47; in a place 15,16; in a plate 20; in the
provinces 17; in the prow 44; in a public garden 20; in the ring
46; in the roads (naut.) 47; in a savings book 47; in a, the sea
17; in the sky 17; in the snow 47; in a spot 15, 16; in a square
46; in a stable 14; in the stern 44; in the street 20, 46; in a
studio 20; in the sun 50; in a tree 47; in a vehicle 11, 48; in a
village 20; in the window 18; in the world 19; in the yard 13.

TIME

In an age 34; in (old) age 25, 52; in babyhood 25; in a
century 24; in childhood 25; in (the) days 24, 35; in the early
hours 86; in the evenings 117; in the future 24; in a half 25;
in the holidays 51; in the interval 24; in the life time 123; in
the middle 24; in a millennium 24; in a minute 52; in a month,
months 24, 34, 52; in the mornings 117; in the past 24; in a
period 25, 35; in the present 24; in a quarter 25; in a reign 123;
in a round 25; in a season 25, 34; in time 128; in (their) time
52; in historic times 35; 'time taken' 35, 36, 80; in the war 36;
in a week, weeks 34, 61; in a year, years 24, 34, 52, 61; in
youth 25.

CLIMATE (in the rain ..) 35, 50, 83, 85.

CAUSE (in a panic ..) 22, 119. STATE (in order, anger ..) 22.
PURPOSE (in defence, proof ..) 39-40.

In the absence 36, 75; in accordance 116; in answer 40; in
the attempt 123; in care 50; in case of 59; in a circle 31; in the
circumstances 124; in comparison with 116; in the course of duty
116; in detail 101; in a dialect 50-51; in exchange 40; in the
face of 110-111; in fact 28, 52; in farewell 60; in favour of 40;
in a gear 51; in harmony 38; in a heap 31; in honour of 40; in
imitation of 87; in intelligence 19; in a manner 64-65; in some
.. measure 27; in memory of 40, 66; in a mirror 37; in a mood 31;
in a number of movements 39; in s.o.'s name 75; in the name of 40;
in the opinion 116; in order 22, 31; in origin 120-121; in the
original 22; in percentages 22; in the picture 31; in power 89;
in practice 22, 50; in the presence of 28, 36, 122; in prospecting
19; in pursuit 32; in revenge 40; in a row 31; in scaffolding 23;
in service 50; in the slightest 28; in a sling 48; in stages 50;
in the grand style 64; in theory 22; in time to 38; in translation
22; in turn 116; in view of 124.

Appear in 21, 27; belief in 37; blind .. in 62; complicity
in 27; consist in 26; cook .. in 49; covered in 22-23; detect in
75-76; disappear in 21; disappointed in 26; doubt in 26; dressed
in 29; end in 100; hide in 21; injection in 36; interest in 92;
lock in 21; lose faith in 26; lucky in 66; the only .. in 63;
place in 21; plunged in 31; pride in 79; settle in 21; show in 53;
sit in 21; specialise in 53; specialist in 120; take part in 27;
whisper in 30; wounded in 36.

Arm in arm 86; comrade in arms 120; hand in hand 78; just in
case 59; make one's way in the world 33.

IN FRONT OF (also fig.) 109-111, 122.

INTO

PLACES 29, 30, 77, 116.

Into the air 29–30; into the attic 54; into bed 30; into the cold, rain .. 66; into the country 77; into the fields 30; into the light 30; into a vehicle 29; into the world 30.

Into accord 31; into the attack 32; into commission 31; into conversation 31; into effect 31; into safe keeping 60.

Accept into 32; change into 29; disappear into 21; divide into 61; force into 91; play o.s. into 101; translate into 66.

Wind wool into balls 31.

NEAR 83, 85, 89, 122.

OF

CAUSE (die of ..) 72, 95   DIMENSION (size of ..) 38
OF A LARGER NUMBER (one of ..) 43.

Accusation, accuse of 26; ascent of 54; ashamed of 110; assurance, assure of 26; battle of 122; born of 94; capable of 57; complain of 56; concept of 107; confession of 26; consist of 43; container of 126; control of 85, 103; conviction of 26; convince of 26; cure of 96; a current of 39; displacement of 39; dispose of 96; a dream of 107; expect of 70; family of (2, 3 ..) 39; fear of 110; game of 37; get rid of 95; guilty of 26; invasion of 55; jealousy of 92; a jump of 38; the key of 94; lack of 26; a letter of 95; maintenance of 74; make of (cloth ..) 43; make fun of 104; the night of 62; observation of 74; the price of 62; pursuit of (including fig.) 74; the question of 107; recollection of 107; remind of 107; repent of 26; review of 56; speak ironically of 104; speed of 39; sure of 26; suspect of 26; suspicion of 26; temperature of 39; test of 59; thought of 107; trial of 103; typical of 99; view of 55; vow of 26.

Film of the novel 117; letter of complaint 127; means of livelihood 91.

OFF

Off the cuff 72; off the street 67.
Work, operate off 94.

ON

PLACES, BUILDINGS, AREAS 30, 44–48, 54.

On a, the bed 15, 19, 30; on the deck 44; on the field(s) 18; on a floor 44; on a planet 47; on a plate 20; on (the) sea 17; on a, the side(s) 47, 69, 112–113; on the sill 18; on the spot 16; on a stretch 16; on a vehicle 48.

TIME

On a day, days 33, 61, 117; on the eve 86–87; on an evening, evenings 34; on holiday(s) 25, 34, 117; on a morning 34, 61; on a night, nights 34; on an occasion 25; on a shift 36; on the threshold 25.

On the basis 49; on behalf of 79; on business 118; on a chain 55; on a channel 116; on a circuit 50; on one's conscience, mind 53; on crutches 49, 55; on a diet 49, 55; on drugs 49; on a frequency 47; on hinges 48; on intuition 120; on a journey .. 32; on a lead 49; on the line 47; on to the offensive 32; on a pension 50, 55; on principle 43; on the radio 47, 116; on reconnaissance

102; to the last detail .. 101-102; to the detriment 40; to dic-
tation 86; to the eye 63; to a gloss 101; to the left, right 113;
to pieces 61; to s.o.'s pleasure .. 93; to the point of 100-102;
to the roots of one's hair 101, 112; to the skin 102; to taste
117; to the teeth 101; to one's underwear 101; to the words 64.

Adapt to 93; address question to 91; agree to 65; an answer
to 65; apologise to 109; appeal to 111; attached to 122; change
down to 66; close to 122; cold to 128; confess to 26; crawl to
111; devote energies to 57; door to 29; do wrong to 109; drink
to 66; due to 72, 82, 118, 119; happen to 127; honest to 111;
incite to 59, 92; induce to 92; key to 92; marriage to 52; married
to 73; path to 91; pay attention to 65; pretend to 110; promote
to 32; raise voice to 56; react to 65; reduce to 87, 100; reduce,
smash, tear to 31; report back to 110; resort to 57; respond to
65; responsible to 110; the right to 62; say goodbye to 126; side-
ways on to 91; testify to 26; visit to 91.

Call to arms 85; call to order 92; come to trial 109; drive
to despair 31; face to face 91; go to expense .. 57; starve to
death 72; take to one's heels 32.

TOWARDS
    PLACE 91.   TIME 86.   ATTITUDE 92, 110-111, 128.
    Arrogant towards 111; direct towards 59; direct efforts
towards 57.

UNDER
    PLACES 83, 85.   STATE (under arrest ..) 83-84, 85.
    Under compulsion 88; under crops 83, 85; under an economic,
social system 123; under way 17.

UNTIL 100.

UP TO 100, 112.

WITH
    TOGETHER, CONTACT .. 126. CAUSE (weep with fear ..) 72, 95.
    TROUBLE WITH .. 127-128.
    With the aid .. 124-125, 127; with the approval 72; with the
best will in the world 124; with the consent 72; with an exception
76; with fasteners 48; with intensity 39; with interest .. 127;
with a small, capital letter 71; with a lining 48; with money 64;
with a parting 65; with permission 72; with pleasure 127; with a
purpose 127; with zippers 48.

    Affable with 128; agree with 126; angry with 57; begin with
71; cope with 127; curry favour .. with 111; fish with 64; frank
with 128; get on with 22; indignant with 57; in love with 37;
make with (ingredients) 49; reproach with 26; secure with 64;
share with 126; stay with 89; vexed with 57; weighed down with 53.

    With (= in view of) her charm .. 124.

WITHIN
    Within memory 52.

NOTE For constructions which have no prepositional equivalent in
English, see, for example pages, 24, 33, 34, 52, 61 (temporal
meanings), 38 (dimensional), 113-114, 117-118 (distributive),
23, 56, 77 (distance), 35 (recurrence), 41 (multiples), 62-
63 (quantification), etc.

Some of these constructions involve verbs such as:-
Adopt 60; answer 65; ask 90; attempt suicide 65; avenge 80;
avoid 39, 96; board 55; borrow 40; by-pass 40; chase 74;
clench 31; climb (hill) 30; confound 31; confront 109; control 103; counter 40; court 74; delight 31; deny 27; despair
30; divorce 126; doubt 26; duplicate 51; embarrass 31; ex-
ceed 78; fail 51; fine 63; follow 74; greet 126; handle 127;
have 89; hit 36; hunt 65, 74; influence 65; leave 68, 94;
lend 40; lock 64; make bargain 57; mark 40; marry 31, 52,
77; match 38; mention 107; miss 118; mock 104; mount 55;
need 26; observe 74; paint 37; panic 31; parachute 51; pay
117; play 37, 51; please 40; prosecute 85; realise 27;
refuse 95; renounce 96; report 56; resemble 64; resist 111;
skate 48; ski 48; slander 56; speak 50; sponsor 103; study
to be 58; supervise 74; survive 23; swear 26; take risk 57;
treat 92, 128; type 51; wear (be wearing) 12.

Other words and phrases rendered in Russian by prepositional constructions include:- Abroad 73, 77; all ears,
eyes 39; boxing champion 120; Centigrade 117; (anti)clock-
wise 117; cello case 94; divorce law 107; downhill 68, 85;
downstairs 115; downstream 115; driving licence 60; driving
test 58; entry permit 60; (un)fortunately 93; heart trouble
127; if I were you 17; just to be on the safe side 59; just
to make sure 97; meal voucher 60; murder case 107; outside
13, 20, 50; petrol coupons 60; plane disaster 127; produc-
tion plan 120; rouble's worth 63; students' hostel 98;
tomorrow's homework 62; trouble is that 25; s.o.'s turn 75;
uphill 30, 68; upstream 115; what a ... 81.

For constructions with 'as' ('as a pledge', 'adapt as'
..), see, for example, pages 23, 32, 33, 39, 40, 41, 65,
75, 80, 86, 87, 97.

* * *

Certain items which do not appear in the index can be
traced thematically. Thus, 'in neutral' appears together
with 'in gear' (p. 51), 'lame, deaf in' together with 'blind
in' (p. 62), 'hatred for' together with 'love for' (p. 92),
'jeer at' together with 'laugh at' (p. 104), 'mourning for'
together with 'grieve for' (p. 118), and so on.